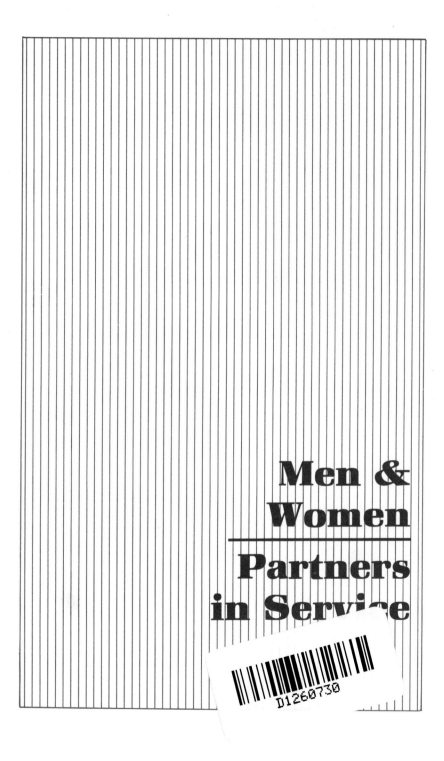

Men &
Women

Partners
in Service

D1260730

Men &
Women

Partners
in Service

Gordon J. Spykman
and Lillian V. Grissen

Library of Congress Cataloging in Publication Data

Spykman, Gordon J.
  Men and women.

  1. Women in church work—Christian Reformed Church. I. Grissen,
Lillian V., 1922–
II. Title.
BV4415.S68   262'.145731   81-18177
ISBN 0-933140-36-3   AACR2

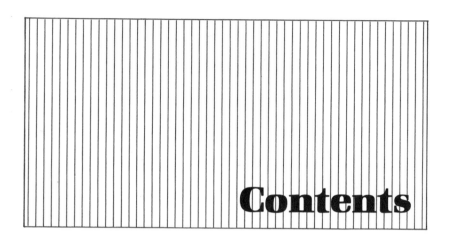

Contents

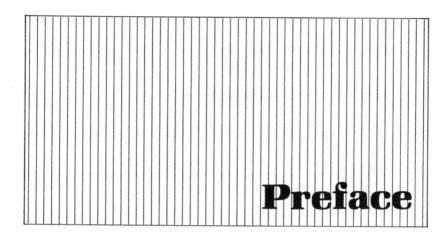

Preface

This book is addressed to a limited audience for a definite purpose. It is written for adults and young adults in the Christian Reformed Church who are concerned about the issue of women serving in the offices of the church (particularly, in the office of deacon). It is written to present, simply and clearly, the primary questions that have risen in the church regarding this issue and the general conclusions reached about them by the study committees appointed by the Synod of the Christian Reformed Church. It is offered with the hope that this presentation will encourage profitable discussion, serve to heal the differences that exist within the church, and promote a unified and unifying solution to this issue in the church.

Already in 1977 synod urged the Education Department of the Board of Publications to continue developing adult educational materials that would encourage fuller use of women's gifts in the church (*Acts of Synod 1977*, p. 43). During succeeding years the scope of this issue in the church narrowed and focused on the question of women in church office and especially in the office of deacon. Several times the Education Department, in consultation with the Education Committee of the Board of Publications, considered producing a book or study guide on this issue. Each time the concern that such a production would be more harmful than healing, more controversial than educational, led to postponement.

Then early in 1980 the Committee for Women in the Christian Reformed Church presented a proposal to the Education Department regarding educational materials dealing with women serving in the offices of the church. The Education Committee considered this proposal and decided to proceed with the project.

The authors of this book are Dr. Gordon J. Spykman and Mrs. Lillian V. Grissen. Dr. Spykman was, until very recently, a member of the Education Committee. He is professor of religion and theology at Calvin College. Mrs. Grissen is assistant professor in journalism and English at Dordt College. They combine theological acumen and writing skills, educational expertise and editorial perception, sensitivity to the issue and awareness of the diverse forms it takes in various parts of the church. Together they have produced this book which we offer for your study.

It is our hope that this work will be a meaningful contribution, if only in a small way, to a profitable discussion of this issue which so disturbs many in the church. We urge you to read it and discuss the questions it raises in a spirit of Christian love and understanding. May the Lord of the church bring his peace to us all and may all of us, men and women alike, come to serve more fully as partners in his great kingdom enterprise.

Harvey A. Smit
Director of Education

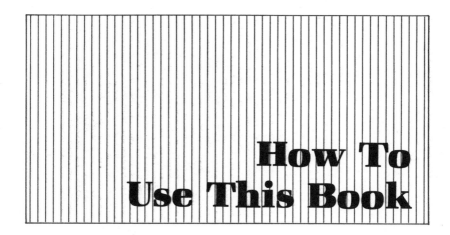

How To Use This Book

There is little to say here that won't become obvious by simply looking at any of the book's chapters. Our intention is that this book be read as the basis for further discussion. That's why the study sessions follow each chapter of the text. Of course the book can be profitably studied by individuals, without the subsequent group discussion. But the very nature of the issue facing us demands that we exchange views with others in the church so that progress toward resolution can be made.

To facilitate good discussion, the study group shouldn't exceed twenty persons since a larger group may prevent members from having opportunities to express their views. Group members must read the assigned chapter(s) before each meeting, and forty-five minutes to an hour should be available for the discussions. To prevent the group from getting bogged down or deadlocked, a leader should be chosen to keep the pace of the sessions going.

A continued atmosphere of Bible study and prayer will help to keep the discussion from deteriorating into expressions of personal prejudice and/or judgment. That's why all the sessions open with Scripture and close with prayer. In addition many of the discussion questions themselves are concerned with the interpretation of the Word.

Any study of this kind should conclude with evaluating what was accomplished and setting new directions for action. "Where do we go from here?" is a question we hope this book and your discussions will help answer.

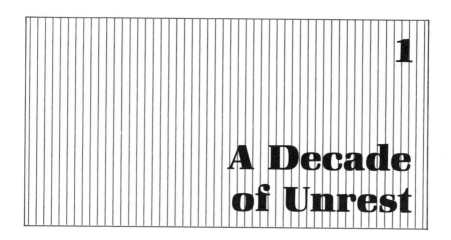

A Decade of Unrest

During recent years no other issue has appeared on the agenda of the Christian Reformed Church so regularly, so vigorously, as the so-called "women's issue." Forceful, even heated, debate has taken place over coffee cups, in church periodicals, in numerous study committees, and on the floor of synod. Thus it is not without reason that the 70s have been called "a decade of unrest" in the church.

Just what is this "women's issue"? As the title of this study guide suggests, it's a debate about the relative positions of men and women in the church, about equality and partnership, about qualifications for church office.

At first glance such a discussion may seem unnecessary. After all, hardly anyone denies that in Christ men and women are equal, or that men and women *together*, as members of the church, are Christ's bride. So why all this fuss about equality? Doesn't it remind you of those silly men who jockeyed for position during those precious moments with Jesus at their last supper together? Who of them, they argued, would be greatest? Jesus answered them succinctly: "You want to be so great? Then don't sit at the table; wait on it!" (Luke 22:26–27).

People writhe and moan in pain, hunger, poverty, and injustice from San Francisco to New York, from Alberta to Florida, from Calcutta to El Salvador, from Sierra Leone to Bangladesh. Their cries rise to heaven! Shouldn't we stop arguing about equality and spend more time striving to relieve the hurting millions, thus using our united energy to demonstrate Christ's mercy to all who are without? Fighting within a church is so debilitating.

Isn't it better to just leave the whole question alone? After all, many men don't seem to care that much, and many women prefer the status quo. Why not ignore the issue? Maybe it will go away! Or maybe—somehow—the problem will solve itself. Or maybe our children won't find the matter so unsettling or biblically questionable, and they can solve it with love and understanding. Let them take care of the matter.

"Generals never die; they just fade away," may be true of the military, but, fortunately or unfortunately, depending on which side you are, it's not true of a controversial issue. An issue keeps coming back. It refuses to fade away, and usually it shouldn't because "fading" is often repression, burying, or denial. The issue, with undiminished dynamism, will pop up or explode at another time and setting. So the question of women and their position as equal partners in the church remains very much with all members of the church, men and women.

What shall we *say* about the question?

What shall we, can we, may we, must we *do* about it?

Reasons for this Study

One reason why this book has been written and offered for your consideration is because much of the discussion on the women's issue has been carried on without enough good information—especially about essential biblical teachings. Synod has appointed qualified and dedicated people to study committees. They have spent hours and days reading, researching, discussing, arguing, and writing. There is a wealth of valuable information and insights available in those reports.

But all of it is buried in the *Acts of Synod*. To most church people that means it's virtually unavailable. Synodical reports seem too scholarly, too complicated, and too formidable to read.

This book tries to bring to ordinary laypeople the substance of those studies mandated by synod. It discusses areas where there seems to be general agreement as well as areas where there appears to be intense disagreement; passages and interpretations to which we all nod, "Amen," and passages we puzzle over and tend to interpret in very different ways.

For many the women's issue is charged with deep emotion. A reasoned, God-honoring solution requires both a Christian spirit of understanding and knowledgeable discussion. This book attempts to provide the information and framework for such study.

History's Heroines

Women have played a major role in redemptive history. They appear in all phases of the biblical drama: the creation, the fall, the building of the Old Testament kingdom, the whole story of Christ, the birth and growth of the church. And they have played every conceivable part: mother, song leader, judge, prophetess, military leader, queen, heroine, follower, student, deaconess.

Because their contributions have been so significant, the names of certain women stand out. Some of them took part in the unfolding of the biblical drama:*

Old Testament	New Testament
Eve	Mary, mother of Jesus
Sarah	Elizabeth
Miriam	Mary Magdalene
Deborah	Mary and Martha
Ruth	Priscilla
Huldah	Phoebe
Esther	Eunice
	Lois

Others have contributed (and continue to contribute) to the growth and development of Christ's church:*

Monica	Johanna Veenstra
Joan of Arc	Mother Teresa
Suzanne Wesley	Tena Huizinga
Queen Wilhelmina	Ruth Vander Meulen

It's important to recognize the roles these women have played. Not to look carefully at both the women and the roles ignores in a large measure the way God uses women. Looking at women's roles, on the other hand, may provide

---

*See Appendix B for brief biographies.

richer understanding of women as equals with men in the church today.

Today's Clamor

The push for human rights and women's rights has been vociferous, urgent, even strident during the past several years. In fact, the radicals of the movement have sometimes been so demanding that certain Christians have disallowed any legitimacy at all to their claim for equal civil rights.

However, in spite of the rather unfortunate manner in which secular organizations have pushed for the liberation of women, many Protestant churches have decided that some of the rights women are clamoring for are legitimate. Such churches have ordained women as deacons, elders, and ministers.

Other churches, including the Christian Reformed Church, have hesitated, continuing to struggle with the issue, its implications, and its foundations. Already in 1957 women were an issue at the Christian Reformed Church Synod. That year delegates officially adopted the policy of *allowing* women to vote at congregational meetings. (See Appendix A.) They did not require consistories to comply.

To date, some churches have implemented that decision; others have not. Some think that historically the time is now ripe to move another step, a decisive step that will enable women to give further service to the church; others do not. And the reports emanating from study committees reflect this disagreement. One person said, upon leaving synod, "I'm beginning to feel like a yo-yo."

In 1968 the Reformed Ecumenical Synod (of which the CRC is a member) asked the church to respond to questions on the women's issue. The church has been working on an answer ever since. After slow, methodical, and careful deliberation, various study committees gave synod lengthy, detailed, carefully grounded majority and minority reports in 1973, 1975, and 1978. One common thread, the Bible's voice on the use of women's gifts in the church, runs through the reports.

Again in 1979 and 1981 the issue appeared, but at these synods the focus was narrowed. The debate concentrated on women as deacons. Is that what "equality" permits? Requires? Denies? Prohibits? No fewer than six reports on the question were presented to synod.

What happened? Synod appointed another committee, this time to study one word—*headship*—as used in the Bible.*

The issue, it seems, will not die. Indeed, it seems that responsible Christians, particularly members of the Christian Reformed Church, should, as men and women in the Lord, promote a forum for constructive discussion of this issue.

And such discussion is being carried on. Various church periodicals have been printing articles *pro* and *con* on women in office. Books and study guides are appearing with varying perspectives. Consistories are considering what individual congregations should or should not do. And a group of concerned women have formed the Committee on Women in the Christian Reformed Church; they are working diligently on the issue, seeking a way to use women's talents and training in equal partnership with men in the church.

This book is a modest attempt to present to the church the substance of what the church's committees have said on this issue. It seeks to promote a profitable, biblical, and healing discussion—one in which with open minds and hearts, with continuing prayer and mutual Christian love, we can perhaps come to some essential understanding of the problem and hopefully to agreement on the answer.

Where Do You Stand on This Issue?

Although the issue itself is not fuzzy, the positions church members and officials take (no fewer than six reports in 1981, remember?) intrude upon one another.

A quick reading and marking of the summary of viewpoints below will demonstrate not only where you stand but also how varied the positions can be. If you don't know where you stand on this issue, aren't you glad you have this opportunity to study it?

---

*This report due at synod in 1983.

Attitude Survey

Directions: Circle the number which is nearest your present position or feeling about women.

	Agree vigorously	Agree moderately	Neither agree nor disagree	Disagree mildly	Disagree vigorously
1. All ecclesiastical offices should, in principle, be open to qualified women as well as men.	1	2	3	4	5
2. The church should make fuller use of women's gifts and talents in the life of the church and the Christian community.	1	2	3	4	5
3. The church should move in the direction of a mediating position, namely to declare the office of deacon open to women, provided this office is clearly distinguished from that of elder or minister.	1	2	3	4	5

4. Even though the principle is right, the church is not ready to accept such a change, and therefore no action should be taken at this time.

    1   2   3   4   5

5. A distinction should be made between "restricted consistory" (composed of ministers and elders, men only) and the "general consistory" (embracing also the diaconate, men and women included).

    1   2   3   4   5

6. The diaconate (men and women) should be separate from the consistory (men only) and fulfill the ministry of Christian mercy only. Further, the diaconate is accountable to the consistory as the ruling body of the church.

    1   2   3   4   5

7. Only men are and should be eligible for ecclesiastical office.

    1   2   3   4   5

Study Session

First

In discussing a sensitive topic of this nature, people are bound to disagree with each other, sometimes perhaps heatedly. With this in mind an opening reading of 1 Corinthians 13 is appropriate, as is a prayer for the presence of the Spirit in all your discussions.

Second

Spend a few minutes reviewing the results of the attitude survey. Go through each item and poll the class to find out where each person stands. Reflect together on the range of differences within your group. Where are you closest? Where widely separated? Do group members agree that a change in their positions is possible?

Third

Select from among the following questions for discussion:

1. Is it important for you as a laymember to know where you stand on an issue such as this? Or will the matter be settled eventually by ministers and elders, regardless of where you stand? Explain.

2. To what extent—and how—will women approach this issue differently than men? Explain.

3. If consistories are studying the issue, what part may laymembers play in the study? Should laymembers—in-

cluding women—contribute? Should they tell the consistories where they stand and why?

4. Rank the following with respect to their importance
   in helping the church resolve this issue (#1 would be
   more important, #5 least important):
   ____Christian tradition—past practices of the church
   ____the pressures of our culture for women's rights
   ____emotions
   ____the Bible's teachings
   ____the findings of synodical study committees

5. Can your group reach a consensus on an overall goal
   for your study of this issue? What is your purpose for
   meeting together?

Fourth

Conclude with this prayer:

Father,
in heaven and in our hearts.
Alpha and Omega.
Teacher, Servant, Helper.
Our Savior, our Lord.
We are
what you have designed,
illumined
by your grace.
Illume our minds.
We confess
that we earn naught
but your rebuke.
Spirit so holy, tutor of souls,
illumine our hearts,
we pray.
That in bearing your image
we mirror well
love and unity,
servanthood and service.
Amen.

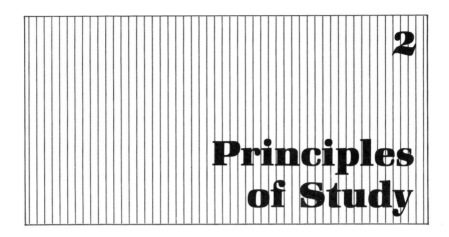

Principles of Study

An issue does not announce its appearance in a church with the pomp and ceremony that herald the approach of the Queen of England. Until about thirty years ago issues usually came to the Christian Reformed Church as matters to be adjudicated or settled. Synod dealt with such issues as a court of law settles cases brought before it. Only in recent years have synods been asked to respond to questions and provide guidelines before a test case arises.

Today an issue appears in neither regal nor legal attire. It approaches more like the sprouting seed blooming unexpectedly. A thought, an idea, a request, or a suggestion is planted. It grows in coffee-cup chatter, articles in the church press, stirrings among women and men, consistory discussions and overtures. Then, suddenly, it's a full-blown issue—an issue that synod must resolve. It's possible that in a still-to-be-written history of the Christian Reformed Church the issue of men and women as equal partners in his church will be seen as a watershed in the denomination's development.

No church enjoys issues; too often heat replaces light, opinions overwhelm facts, personalities dwarf principles, and politics outmaneuver progress toward a spiritual decision. But issues must be settled, and settling them depends not just on how participants think but also on how they feel. It's a fact that emotions frequently and often conclusively affect and effect problem-solving. Still, as Christians, we should act, should base our decisions, not on opinions or feelings but on *truth.* With that we all agree. But even though we all follow the same One—who is *truth*—and believe the same divinely inspired Word of *truth,* we find at times that we don't agree. It seems that our understandings of truth differ.

That's partly because our perceptions of truth are imperfect. We "see in a mirror dimly" and "know in part" (1 Cor. 13:12). And it's partly due to our different experiences and viewpoints. Six witnesses to the same accident may all swear in court and be sure they're telling the truth of what they've seen, yet their versions of it may sound like six different accidents.

Still, we believe that the truth is greater than our understandings or perceptions of it. If we listen in faith to God's Word and Spirit and in love to our fellow believers, the truth will shape the issue's final solution.

The harvest of an issue, of course, is its resolution and the implementation of its solution in furthering the spiritual growth of the church. Before the harvest must come the study, and to study profitably one must know where to begin and how to study.

The Church Makes a Survey

Already in 1914 and 1916, synod, still conducting business in the Dutch language, dealt with matters concerning women. But it was not until 1970 that synod appointed a committee (specifically) "to examine in the light of Scripture the general Reformed practice of excluding women from the various ordained offices in the church." That biblical study was followed in 1973 by another committee mandated "to receive and evaluate the reactions of the churches and to [present] a report to the Synod of 1975."

The 1973 committee followed its mandate by placing a request for reactions in *The Banner,* the denominational weekly which reaches approximately 45,000 homes. They received a "very gratifying" 165 responses—133 from councils or consistories and 22 from individuals. The committee drew the following conclusions from the replies:

1. The overwhelming majority in the Christian Reformed Church is not of a mind to open the existing ecclesiastical offices to women.
2. There is support for instituting the office of deaconess,

although this office is not clearly defined.

3. There is considerable concern that the church make all possible use of women in the work of the church outside the existing offices.

Reflecting on these conclusions and their basis in the survey, one could—and perhaps should—raise some critical questions. How valuable is such a survey? The responses don't indicate why councils, consistories, and individuals reacted as they did. They show a concern about the issue, but little more. And what do terms like *overwhelming majority* or *considerable concern* mean when, first of all, the responses were from a minority of the churches and individuals contacted, and second, the issue is one that should be decided by *truth,* not by opinions and ideas current in the churches.

But concerned church members, responding to the committee's conclusions, have asked some even deeper questions. Some pertinent points they have raised are:

1. *Do the original creation ordinances given Adam and Eve still hold for us today? Will a close look at God's fundamental revelation in creation help us to better understand the man–woman relationship today?*

Article II of the Belgic Confession calls God's creation an "elegant book, wherein all creatures, great and small" reveal God's power and divinity. The late Louis Berkhof, former professor of theology at Calvin Seminary, claimed that general revelation is addressed to humanity simply "as the creature and image bearer of God." It does not come to us verbally, but rather embodies "divine thought in the embodiment of nature, in the general constitution of the human mind...in the voice of conscience...and in the lives of individuals in particular." What does this "creation" book say concerning the issue?

2. *What effects did and does sin have upon our understanding of God's original will for our life together as male and female in partnership in his world?*

Article XV of the Belgic Confession tells us: "We believe that through the disobedience of Adam original sin is extended to all mankind; which is a corruption of the whole nature and a hereditary disease, wherewith even infants in their mother's womb are infected, and which produces in man all sorts of sin, being in him as a root thereof, and therefore is so vile and abominable in the sight of God that it is sufficient to condemn all mankind." How does sin distort the issue?

3. *What bearing does the Bible have on this question? Will a study of pertinent texts help us arrive at a right solution?*

At first this question seems ridiculous, improper, and not worth answering. As Christians and a Christian church, of course we must turn to the Bible. Doesn't John Calvin teach that the Scriptures are our "spectacles" which correct our sin-blurred vision? How can we regain a right understanding of how we are to live together in love as believing men and women in the church, except in the light of God's Word?

But these questions raise a valid point. A haphazard method of seeking answers from the Bible can be, and sometimes is, worse than no Bible study at all. Think, for example, of those who claim the Bible teaches that medically needed blood transfusions are forbidden.

We certainly need the Bible, the indispensable "spectacles." All of us are bothered by more or less distorted spiritual vision. Heaven may astonish us when it reveals God's perfect truth to us in full, but here on earth we seem often to distort the very Word that is intended to correct our distortions. May we expect the Holy Spirit to reveal the truth of the Word to us when we approach it in a wrong way and with inferior methods?

The preceding are some of the questions that surfaced in the church when the initial synodical study committee's reports failed to result in a clear solution of the issue, acceptable to the majority.

The Need for Principles of Biblical Interpretation

In view of the questions posed in the preceding section, it's not surprising that synod realized very early in the history of this issue that different points of view on men and women as equal partners in the church and on the use of women's gifts in the church were rising out of different ways of understanding and interpreting the Bible. Believers, equal in their willingness to let the Bible dictate a resolution and equally convinced of the soundness of their interpretation, were coming up with different answers.

How did the church face this impasse? In 1975 synod appointed "The Committee on Hermeneutical Principles Concerning Women in Office"—an impressive title for a group with an important task. "Herman who?" you ask. *Hermeneutics* comes from a Greek word meaning "to translate, explain, or interpret." Therefore, we understand <u>*hermeneutics*</u> to mean simply "<u>interpretation of Scripture."</u>

Seminaries offer courses in hermeneutics to would-be ministers. And these courses are necessary. Interpreting the Bible is not as simple as it first appears. Carelessness, superficiality, preconceived notions, haste, eclecticism, bias, sentimentality, intellectualism, liberalism, prejudice—all can and do distort meaning. Bible scholars who know the meaning of words in the original are often appalled by the frequency with which many preachers force relevance on a text by interpreting words in a way never intended by the inspired author.

And preachers are not the only ones guilty of poor hermeneutics. Many Bible readers want to "read it as it is." They insist that too much emphasis on interpretation minimizes illumination by the Spirit. And they're partially right. An open mind and heart *are* necessary. Otherwise we'll stumble into the same problems as the freshman student asked to research both sides of an issue for her term paper. After two weeks of hard work she hurried to her professor's office in dismay: "I started out *knowing* marijuana should be legalized because everybody uses it. But after reading, I'm not so sure."

At the same time, however, we must recognize in our hermeneutics the importance of the true meaning of the text itself. To understand what the biblical authors meant, we must, among other things, interpret their messages in the context of their cultures. And we must understand the flavor and tone of the language they use.

Sometimes that's difficult. Folks of Dutch origin, for example, have difficulty translating the exact meaning of *gezellig, benauwd, deugniet,* and *vreselijk.* Bible translators have the same trouble agreeing about the meaning of many Greek and Hebrew words. Such disagreement and uncertainties have led many Christians to conclude that hermeneutics should be reserved for the minister. But that's not so. Without labeling it as such, people employ hermeneutics whenever they determine the meaning of any speech or writing. For example, the last painful days and tense hours before the release of the American hostages in Iran were spent in interpreting the precise and implied exchange of messages between two governments. Government leaders were employing hermeneutics. And like them, we often need to interpret before we can understand.

Admittedly, that's not easy. And there's no magic formula for easy Bible study either. To interpret the Bible correctly the reader must attempt to understand the rural context in which most of the Bible was written and must research the ideas and customs of the ancient culture in which the Bible's authors lived. One who lives in a rural section of North America, for example, can relate to the rural sheep-herding or agricultural illustrations of the Bible better than a big-city dweller can. An impoverished ghetto resident will understand Jesus' innumerable comments on the poor and rich better than the wealthy suburbanite does.

But at the same time the reader must recognize that the message of the Bible transcends the era in which it was written. The Bible is always contemporary and up-to-date. And to interpret it fully the reader must also be a contemporary person, open and sensitive to dilemmas and problems of to-day—in this case, the longing of Christian women to be equal partners with men in serving Christ and his church and to use their gifts in the church fully and completely. The reader, "living" in those two worlds, must see that the two worlds come together, become one, through and in Christ.

Each generation has the task of reinterpretation. We are not asked to believe that the last word concerning men and women, equality and partnership in the church, was set in stone by the end of the first century. In the light of what continues to happen in the explosion of human knowledge, would it make sense to interpret and impose a principle in identical fashion in every century? If it did, would we Christians today be putting lightning rods on our homes and church buildings (once considered a sign of mistrust in divine providence) or be driving cars to church on Sunday (once strictly forbidden except perhaps for a visiting pastor)?

We can thank our Reformation leaders, Martin Luther and John Calvin, for returning to believers the right to study the Bible for themselves rather than to have the church dictate the interpretation for them. Before the Reformation the church had buried the life-giving meaning of texts under heavy tradition and interpretation. It seemed impossible to get at the essential message; the Bible was merely the sounding board for the establishment.

Luther stripped away all the excess baggage that the established church had added over the centuries and now found "justification by faith only." The Bible was for people who wanted to hear God, not merely the church, speak. The Bible, said the reformers, is greater than any official interpreter. Believers who study it carefully and prayerfully, paying attention to the creeds and confessions and the preaching of the church, can understand God's Word.

And yet synod deemed it necessary that principles be outlined even for its own select, blue-ribbon study committees! It sounds contradictory, doesn't it? But it is not. Serious Christians desire help in interpretation. It is one of the compelling aspects of God's Word that it demands more of us as we grow in knowledge and faith. The synod and study committees, then, sought to make the Bible more, not less, accessible to those of you who are now studying this issue. They prepared the following list of useful principles to provide a set of common ground rules for all of us to follow:

1. The Bible is authoritative and infallible.
2. The Bible's message is redemption, liberation, and renewal.
3. The Bible, though varied, has organic unity in purpose, and its message develops progressively.
4. The Bible is historical.
5. The Bible's literary and theological elements must be considered.
6. The Bible speaks to its day, both in accommodation and in polemics.
7. The analogy of Scripture (comparison of Scripture with Scripture) is essential.
8. The abiding principles of Scripture must be sepa-

rated from local or cultural applications of a principle.

These are the principles the study committee outlined for guidance in seeking from Scripture an answer to the issue of women in church office. If you find these too brief to be truly helpful, we suggest you turn to Appendix C and read there a longer version of these principles with some explanatory comments.

These are meant to be "guidelines that may be used in the understanding of the passages most often quoted in the matter of admission or non-admission of women to ecclesiastical office" (*Acts of Synod 1978,* p. 487). In our further study of this issue, we'll be trying, in accordance with these principles, to understand the pertinent texts of Scripture.

Study Session

First

Regardless of where we stand on issues, we stand together in our love for the Word of God. Psalm 119 celebrates that Word and asks for guidance in understanding it and living it. For your opening activities today, read—as a prayer—Psalm 119:33–36, 89–91, 103–105, 129–130.

Second

Select from among the following discussion questions, according to time and interest:

1. If it is valid to make a survey in order to "feel the pulse" of a denomination, what factors must be taken into account to insure accurate results? Does the survey quoted in chapter 2 meet your criteria for accuracy?

2. Some say, "Why not read the Bible at face value? All this talk about principles and interpretation is too confusing! It hurts more than it helps." Do you agree? Why or why not?

3. If Bible teaching is so clear when the Bible is studied correctly, why are we divided on issues?

4. Some say that biblical considerations are decisive against women holding office; others insist the Bible is not opposed to women holding any office that men hold in the church. Which of the principles of Bible study do you think are most directly involved in such

differences of opinion?

5. We are all aware that principles are easily forgotten in practice. What has each of the following speakers substituted for sound principles?

Speaker A: "It worked in the old days. The Bible doesn't change. So it ought to be good enough today."

Speaker B: "Of course, women should hold office with men. They can do the work just as well as men."

Speaker C: "We can't be dragging our feet on this issue. Look around—it's obvious that secular society is miles ahead of the church. It's high time we catch up."

6. Supposing synod someday soon makes a decision contrary to your position on this issue of women in office. What attitude should you have and what action should you take toward your denomination?

Third

Are there other reactions or comments that members of the group wish to make? Perhaps several individuals could sum up what they take to be the main point of chapter 2. Then close with prayer. A suggested prayer:

Father,
we think of Pentecost
when men and women
of many nations
heard many tongues,
each his own,
each her own,
with no interpreter.
We marvel
at the wonders of our tongues,
    voices,
    minds,
    spirits.
Help us to see
the beauty
of your Word
which is its own interpreter.
Amen.

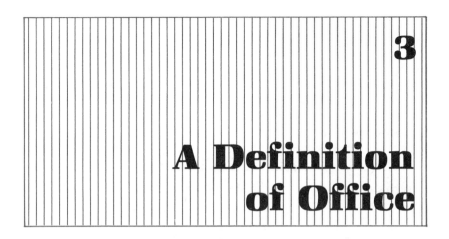

A Definition of Office

3

As children many of us tried to make time go faster in church by wondering: Why did the minister need three soft chairs? Why did he first use the chair on the left and then the chair on the right, but never the one in the middle? Why did he take a drink of water rather than a peppermint at precisely the same juncture of the seemingly endless morning worship? Why did certain men (elders and deacons) walk in and sit in the front of the church? Why were elders so very old and deacons almost as old? Why weren't there any women in front with those men?

As we sit in church today, Sunday after Sunday, follow the printed liturgy (actively or passively as the case may be), watch the elders march in (if they do), note the deacons take (or perhaps, accept) the offering, watch the children drop in coins (or paper) with varying gestures of charm or curiosity—do we ever wonder why we do as we do? Why is the procedure so comfortably similar no matter in which congregation we find ourselves?

And would it be comfortable to others? Would young New Testament Christians recognize our church? Probably. The gospel has not changed; the good news then is the good news now. Yet, at the same time, the twentieth-century church is not the first-century church. Much of what we say or sing and practice is not as scripturally *bound* as we often think it is. Because we want to be true to the biblical principles we confess and because tradition, in the case of our Christian practices and customs, is a very dear first cousin to Scripture, confusion and questionable overlapping do occur occasionally.

The Report on Ecclesiastical Office and Ordination (1973) helps us understand where and how some of this confusion has occurred in the issues related to women in church offices. It provides both a biblical analysis and historical review of office and ordination, showing how office is related to authority and service in the church.

Office Means Service

In the report the synodical study committee drew several conclusions. Let us look at some of them.

> *The term for office in the Greek New Testament is* diakonia, *meaning "service" or "ministry." In this basic sense ecclesiastical office is one and indivisible, for it embraces the total ministry of the church, a ministry that is rooted in Christ.* *

The Greek word *diakonos* is masculine. Still that does not mean that in New Testament times only men filled ecclesiastical offices. Even as the German language considers all nouns to be feminine, masculine, or neuter, but does not imply that the object named by the noun is the same gender as the noun, so also with Greek. A masculine ending does not prove the sex of the person labeled.

The translators of the Bible appear to have had difficulty translating this term *diakonos*. In the King James Version of the New Testament it becomes "minister" twenty times, "deacon" three times, and "servant" seven times.

The writers of the Old Testament had no word that carried the meaning of *office* as we understand it today. Yet the King James translation of the Old Testament uses the English word "office" thirty times, even though in only ten cases is it the direct translation of a Hebrew word. It is also curious that in the New Testament a Greek word corresponding to our idea of office is missing. Instead the word *diakonia*, meaning "service," is commonly used.

Still we should remember that an exactly corresponding word is not absolutely necessary. The idea of office is as deeply imbedded in the Bible as the concept of the Trintiy,

---

*Words in italics are quoted from the *Acts of Synod 1973*, pages 713–14.

another word which doesn't appear in the Scriptures.

It's also interesting to note that nowhere, in either Testament, does the word translated in English as office connote prestige or exalted status (*Acts*, 1975). This is remarkably in keeping with Jesus' teaching that he who would be first shall be last.

This comprehensive ministry (office) is universal, committed to the whole church, not to a select group of individuals within the church. The task of ministry is shared by all and is not limited to a special, professional class. The ministry of the church is Christ's ministry, shared by all who are in Christ.

The Old Testament priesthood, one of the first offices, pointed to Christ, the Mediator. But with the outpouring of the Holy Spirit, all we who are in Christ have become "a chosen race, a royal priesthood" (1 Pet. 2:9). It isn't hard to imagine why this question of priesthood became a gargantuan issue among the Jews and Jewish Christians. Imagine laymen or laywomen saying to those regal Levites, that special-privilege group, "We too are priests." Any reference to the Old Testament civil and ceremonial laws could easily and certainly demonstrate the heresy of priesthood for all God's people it would seem.

But the outpouring of the Holy Spirit made an undeniable change. As Luther and Calvin rightly declared in the sixteenth century, Christ had fulfilled his work of redemption and mediation for all time. No longer were the priests of the Roman Catholic church required to mediate for humanity to God. The priesthood is shared by all believers.

Special Ministries within the Church

It is not inconsistent with this universal office-sharing, and it is in keeping with apostolic practice, that some individuals within the church be appointed to certain special tasks. The Scriptures report a setting apart to special ministries or service. Both in the Old and New Testaments God calls particular people for particular tasks.

The concept of ordered tasks and services is apparent as early as the time of Moses and Aaron. Aaron (Ex. 28:1) was appointed to the special ministry as mediator between God and the people. It was a very specific task and at that time God wouldn't tolerate anyone usurping Aaron's priestly duties (Lev. 10:1–2; 2 Chron. 26:18).

We see this necessity of order and assigned tasks also among people who believe communal living is the best way to demonstrate the love of Jesus; sooner or later they discover that functions and tasks must be assigned. A busy mother of several children knows that everyone's responsibility simply means nobody's responsibility.

God's sense of order is perfect. Space scientists and technicians can command *Voyager II* cameras to take pictures of Saturn only because God's time, laws, and principles are dependable. At the same time, scientists who ignore these principles frequently upset the delicate balance of insect–bird–crop life, forgetting that God has assigned specific tasks to each segment of nature, tasks that are needed to maintain his created order and harmony.

Because God ordained order also in the social area of life, he appointed not only priests, but later kings to rule his people. They functioned in the civil arena. He also appointed prophets. Together these prophets, priests, and kings functioned to govern and care for God's people during the Old Testament era. All were types of Christ and their ministries were fulfilled in him. Yet God continued to use people for specified functions also in the New Testament.

Paul frequently enumerated gifts and their uses in specific service (Rom. 12; 1 Cor. 12; etc.). At first the apostles alone were commissioned to spread the good news (Acts 1:8). But when three thousand people were added to the list of believers at Pentecost, the leaders saw the need for special tasks and so they divided the workload. Stephen, the deacon whom we remember for noble martyrdom, also spoke and did wonders (Acts 6:8; 7:1–53). Philip became an evangelist. Barnabas and Saul were called to be missionaries. Elders (Acts 11:30) and prophets (Acts 21:9) ministered to the people. (It's interesting to note that the prophets mentioned in this passage are women.)

In the major disagreement over the relationship between circumcision and salvation, the elders and apostles led the discussion and dialogue, but *all* the believers played a part in reaching a decision (Acts 15:22–29).

*From the beginning these special ministries were func-
tional in character, arising under the guidance of the
Spirit primarily in the interests of good order and effi-
ciency in the church, created as a means to the end of
enabling the church to carry out Christ's work in the
world most efficiently and effectively.*

A survey of the New Testament writings demonstrates
how many different functions were identified as offices in
the early church. Among them were the following:

disciples (in restricted and broader sense)
missionaries (Luke 10:1–20—the seventy who were sent
    out by Christ)
apostles (the twelve original disciples plus others later)
deacons (the seven assigned a special task—Acts 6)
prophets (those who prophesy)
evangelists
teachers
elders and bishops
deacons (besides those in Acts 6)

A summary of the contributions these people made to the
phenomenal growth of the infant church invites us to no-
tice how the Holy Spirit distributes among *all* believers,
through gifts and tasks, the work of advancing his kingdom.

*The special ministries are primarily characterized by
service, rather than by status, dominance, or privilege.
The authority which is associated with the special ministries is an authority defined in terms of love and service.*

The word *diakonia,* meaning "service" or "ministry," is significant to our understanding of office. Yet the definition or
explanation of the word *office* evokes disagreement among
scholars who have studied the issue of men and women as
partners in service.

Jesus himself said, "Let the greatest among you become as
the youngest, and the leader as one who serves. . . . But I
am among you as one who serves" (Luke 22:26–27; see also
Mark 10:35–45). Herein lies the pattern for service and
ministry. The radicalness of Christ's pattern must be con-
trasted with the Greek concept of service. According to the
Greeks only lowly people served; service indicated a low

class in society. Not so, said Jesus. Service is just that—*service*. That alone identifies men and women as Christ's disciples.

The church today often puts more emphasis on the ministry aspects of deacons than on the service requirements that Christ outlined for all offices. And to the word *ministry* we have attached the idea of eminence, authority, and esteem. Or perhaps past practices have ingrained these concepts in us so deeply that we have come to believe that eminence, authority, and esteem are not only traditional but also biblical connotations of the office of minister of the Word. On the other hand, even if the words *minister* and *servant* are synonymous, that doesn't wipe out the need to respect a minister as a special servant of God carrying out a special task in the church. Still, to many the title *Reverend* suggests dignity rather than service. Perhaps to counterbalance that emphasis some of our ministers today are on a first-name basis with their parishioners, or prefer being called "pastor."

The New Testament uses of the word *diakonia* compel us to look at the functionaries of the church (people who hold office) as servants, first of God, then of other people. *Diakonia* doesn't suggest that a church office elevates a person above fellow believers but rather that office describes a specific way in which one may serve.

> *The special ministries of some believers are to be distinguished not in essence but in function from the comprehensive ministry shared by all believers, and distinctions among the special ministries themselves are also functional. There is therefore no essential distinction but only a functional one between ministers, elders, deacons, and all other members of the church. There is a difference in manner of service, but all are commissioned to serve.*

As we trace the meaning and uses of the word *diakonos,* we see clearly that the structure of the church government—namely, elders, preacher(s), and deacons as a council or consistory—is not necessarily correct because of the essence of each office. A study of the word *diakonos* demonstrates that function, rather than essence, marks an office.

Church history does not disclose a clear pattern of church

government in early years. It does, however, reflect diversity in the concept of church order, diversity which progressed into standardization on the basis of organizational models developed at the time. Development of organization arose pragmatically; it rose primarily out of need.

Until the Protestant Reformation, church history reveals the rather haphazard growth in number, distinction, and power of church offices, particularly the bishopric and papacy. The bishops became the guardians of truth and with this responsibility grew their prestige and power. The laity was then clearly distinguishable from the officials. Lost was the New Testament concept of the priesthood of all believers; laymembers, men and women, became second-class citizens.

Then came 1517 and the Protestant Reformation. It was the era of reform—powerful, electrifying, reaching out everywhere. Reformers adopted a new stance on office. The focus of the Reformation was on justification by faith, rather than on church order and office. The Reformers used the term *office* rather loosely. But the phrase "priesthood of all believers" reemerged. Heidelberg Catechism Q & A 32 reads:

But why are you called a Christian?

Because by faith I am a member of Christ and so I share in his anointing. . . .

Perhaps the Reformers did not realize how totally revolutionary this doctrine was. It contradicted tradition on one significant point at least by asserting that the universal priesthood means *all* believers, men and women, are office holders in the church of Jesus Christ and in the Christian community. To "share in his anointing," as the Heidelberg Catechism states it, emphasizes the sharing of Christian men and women in Christ's prophetic, priestly, and kingly office. It is this sharing that makes service, in both the general office of all believers and in the special offices in the church, so possible and compelling.

Because the Scriptures do not present a definitive, exhaustive description of the special ministries (offices) of the church, and because these special ministries as described in Scripture are functional in character, the Bible leaves room for the church to modify its special ministries and adapt them to changing times in order to carry out its service to Christ effectively in all circumstances.

It seems to be true that we accept today's church—its liturgy, government, and interpretations—as the way it has always been and, therefore, as the way it should be. It is necessary, of course, to jealously guard principles based on biblical teaching; we need to do so vigorously and lovingly. We need also to evaluate traditional customs and practices to determine whether Scripture requires them, permits them, or rejects them. Each generation must do so if the church of Christ is to speak clearly and advance the kingdom in the contemporary world.

In analyzing the word *office,* one sees that the New Testament uses descriptive terms such as shepherds, leaders, and guardians in connection with servant, service, or office. Therefore the authority of office may be considered that of "servants." John Calvin, who had a rather high view of church order, also stressed the service aspect of office. His "functionalism allowed him to be somewhat pragmatic and flexible, sensitive to the immediate situation. . .he saw that offices were not an end in themselves, but a means to the end of the building up of the people of God" (*Acts,* 1973).

Study
Session

First

Hebrews 3:1 urges those "who share in a heavenly call [to] consider Jesus, the apostle and high priest of our confession." Reflect for a few moments on how Jesus demonstrated the servanthood nature of office. Perhaps you could read these short passages aloud: Mark 10:41–45, Luke 10: 25–27, and John 13:34–35.

Take a moment, if you wish, to share with one other person an instance from the life of Christ which, to you, speaks of "servanthood."

Second

The seven statements explaining the nature of office are taken from the Report on Ecclesiastical Office and Ordination. Here is a summary of those seven statements, intended to serve as reminders while you discuss chapter 3:

1. *Diakonia* is the equivalent of service or ministry.
2. Ministry is universal; it includes the whole church, all who are in Christ.
3. Some individuals are appointed to certain specific tasks.
4. Special ministries are functional in character.
5. Special ministries are characterized by service, not status.
6. Distinction among church offices lies not in essence but in function.

7. The Bible, being neither definitive nor exhaustive, leaves room for the church to modify its ministries to the times or special conditions.

The following biblical references provide background support for the statements. You may wish to refer to some of these passages as you discuss chapter 3.

Gifts, ministries, appointments:
Acts 1:8, 22, 26; 2:41–43; 3–5; 6:1–8; 7:1–53; 8:34–38; 11:29–30; 13:1–3; 14:14–15, 21–23; 15:6, 22, 32
Romans 12:6–8
1 Corinthians 12:4–11, 28–30
Ephesians 4:11–12

Deacons:
Acts 6:1–6
1 Timothy 3:8–13

Servant concept:
Mark 10:35–45
Luke 22:24–27

Relationship between authority involved in special office and in the office of all believers:
Acts 6:3, 5a
Galatians 2:9
1 Timothy 3:8–10, 12; 4:12–16
2 Timothy 2:15–16, 21–25
Titus 2:1, 7–8
Hebrews 13:7
1 Peter 5:1–3

Third

The word *office* deserves much discussion, more than the few questions below suggest. You may want to spend an extra session on this topic if you have the time and interest. If you have a single session only, select from among the following questions, choosing those of interest to your group:

1. What is the church?
   a. Hierarchy (government by ascending ranks)
   b. Aristocracy (government by nobility or class believed to be best qualified)
   c. Oligarchy (government by the powerful few)

    d. Democracy (government by the people, the majority)

    e. something other than the above

    In deciding which is correct, consider the concepts explained in chapter 3 and defend your answer. How does your answer contribute to a resolution of the women's issue?

2. Are the present offices of minister, deacon, elder, and evangelist as we know them, only functional in nature? Are they also clothed with authority? Should they be? Explain.

3. Has the Christian Reformed Church placed too much emphasis on the distinction between the general office (all believers) and the special offices (deacon, elder, minister, evangelist)? Or not enough? Why?

4. Is there too much (or too little) distinction between the offices of elder and deacon in the Christian Reformed Church today? Explain.

5. Paul emphasizes that each individual should use his or her gifts in the service of or on behalf of all believers. Very often in today's church gifts go unused. For example, sometimes a highly qualified nominee for elder or deacon goes unelected year after year. Why? Should, perhaps, elders and deacons not be elected (which seems too often to be based on popularity)? Should we cast lots or use some other approach?

6. How much has the traditional role assigned to male and female primarily by our culture determined what men and women do in the church? Consider, for example, who teaches church school, who cares for infants or toddlers in church nurseries, who serve as church secretaries, who serve as council/consistory secretaries. If all these tasks are for servants and if *diakonos* (meaning "service" or "ministry") is reserved for men, shouldn't the men be in the above tasks as well? Comment.

7. Acts 6 tells the story of the appointment of the seven "to serve tables" (vv. 2–3). This is usually considered to be the initiation of the office of deacon. Why has the

serving of tables been relegated primarily to women in the church of today?

8. Does the Bible suggest that the church today should have additional offices beyond those of elder, deacon, or minister? If the essence of office is service, shouldn't other positions (such as teaching, for example) be considered offices? Why or why not?

9. Does the priesthood of all believers mean that all offices in the church are open to all believers? Why or why not?

10. Not all members of the synodical study committee agree that functionalism permits flexibility in office. Is there some aspect of office that does not and cannot change from biblical times to the present? Defend your answer.

Fourth

In closing this session the group may wish to recap briefly the essence of office as defined by the synodical study committee. It is well to remember that the definition of office is important as it bears on the issue of men and women as partners in service. It is equally necessary to remember that differences in interpretation shouldn't diminish our oneness in Christ.

Fifth

As part of your prayer we suggest the following paraphrase of John Calvin's prayer found in his commentary on Malachi 2:9.

Almighty God,
you have condescended to choose us as priests;
you chose us when we were not only low,
but foreign, separate, alien from you, your holiness!

Holy Spirit, consecrate us to yourself
so we may be your "holy victims."

Help us always to remember our office, our calling.
Help us devote ourselves to you, to serve you.

We want to give you our work, our effort,
so everyone may see we truly belong to you,
because of your Son.

We recognize that your Son is the highest,
the true priest, continuing forever.
We want to be part of his priesthood,
so he may accept us as fellow workers with himself.
We desire that by our actions your name will be
   glorified,
by Jesus Christ, our head, and all of us who believe.
Amen.

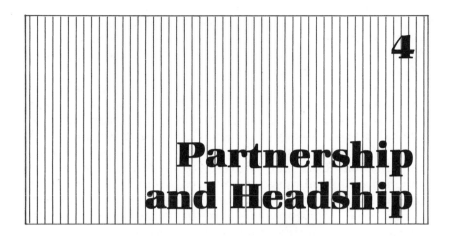

4

Partnership and Headship

Many authors over the centuries have used a framework within which to tell their stories. England's Chaucer, whose *Canterbury Tales* are still very much alive, used a group of pilgrims traveling together to a shrine as his framework. To help pass the time as they slowly plodded along, each pilgrim told a tale to amuse and entertain the others.

Authors also use a specific point of view to tell their tales. A story told from the viewpoint of a teenager, for example, cannot be sprinkled with the experience and sophistication only acquired by forty years of life and living. *Anne Frank's Diary,* the true story of a Jewish family's experience during the Nazi persecution of Dutch Jews in World War II, would lose its honest appeal and single point of view if suddenly an adult would insist on helping Anne write a more sophisticated account of those fear-filled years.

Part of the unmatched beauty of God's Word is its fascinating framework and its divine viewpoint screened through mortal pen. The "story" of the Bible is a mystery unfolding itself. Who could imagine from reading Genesis 3:15 that many centuries later a humble, apparently ordinary man would appear, a man who could and would deliver people from sin? Who could have guessed God's solution to the crime of human sin? Who could ever write a mystery so completely involving the reader that his belief in the solution would enable him to participate in working toward the completion? And where have we ever found an author who directed so many writers to use their own writing style and who employed so many types of literature while retaining unity, singleness of purpose, and his own point of view? That's part of the amazing marvel of God's inspired, infallible Word and the good news it tells.

Further, just as literary critics interpret and critique novels and poems differently, so earnest, serious Christians among us view parts of God's story differently. Different explanations don't necessarily mean inferior or superior interpretations. Yet much agreement of interpretation also exists in the Christian Reformed Church. For example, we agree that the entire biblical message revolves around God's covenantal dealings with humanity and that *creation* ➻→ *fall* ➻→ *redemption* ➻→ *consummation* are the crucial turning points. Agreement about this covenant is as encouraging as it is important.

This is not to say, though, that no problems exist. Some disagreements have been resolved, but an unsolved problem revolves around men and women as *equal* partners in Christian service. The issue seems often to concentrate on the seeming ambiguity of the meaning of male *headship.*

One of the synodical reports states that "progress will not be made in clarifying the possible role of women in the office of elder and minister until a comprehensive study is made by a committee composed of theologians and historians, men and women, on what the Bible says about the relationship between men and women before the fall, after the fall, and after the accomplishment of redemption in Christ." From this statement we can see that it is essential to keep the central purpose of the covenantal story in mind.

As we examine how men and women as partners in Christian service, particularly in the church, are or should be related today, we should keep in mind the development of God's plan in its historical setting:

Stage One   The creation order: man and woman together, perfect covenant partners in God's beautiful world

Stage Two   The effects of the fall: man's and woman's togetherness, the covenantal partnership, devastatingly broken

Stage Three Redemption in Christ Jesus: man's and

woman's partnership restored and renewed in principle

Stage Four Consummation, second advent: man's and woman's partnership perfectly fulfilled in the final renewal of God's original purpose

A look ahead at the chapter titles will indicate that the above story, God's plan, is the pattern chosen for this book.

A Good Beginning

To understand Genesis 1 we may again consider a literary technique—this time one employed in both electronic and written mysteries. You have seen or read a flashback. It occurs when the author depicts a resolution or an ending and then interrupts the picture by showing or telling events that happened earlier.

Because Stage Four is the restoration of creation to what it was intended to be, it can be said, in a sense, that Stage Four is revealed in the first chapter of the Bible. Genesis 1 is a picture of Stage One, the beautiful, perfect universe God created. He will restore this same beauty and perfection in a fulfilled form when he comes again (Stage Four).

Between Stages One and Four are Stages Two and Three, the stages in which the answer to our sinfulness is given through the revealing and unfolding of God's mystery of salvation—a complete cycle. We now live in Stage Three. Though sin is still with us, we are redeemed and liberated, praying "thy kingdom come," and seeking the restoration, in Christ, of this fallen, sin-marred world.

In Our Image

Genesis 1:26–28

The creation of human beings climaxed God's original work of creation. In this superb setting, the then almost completed creation, God created male and female simultaneously, giving them the highest compliment possible: God patterned male and female after himself. It's almost impossible to comprehend the magnitude of God's words in Genesis 1:28: "Let us make man in our image, after our likeness."

But it's important to recognize that male and female *together* share God's image. God introduced the first male and female (vv. 26–28) in a *single* act. And although the male–female distinction is a real, vital part of God's creation, male and female are on an equal footing as images of God, joint heirs of the covenant promises and obligations. What holds for male holds for female. Neither is a silent partner; neither is a second-class citizen; neither is a restricted member.

As a result, both sexes are invested with the office ("service") of believer. Both, as prophets, are to speak prophetically—as God's spokespeople in his world. Both, as priests, are to render priestly service in the temple of creation. Both, as kings, are to serve God's creation.

Together man and woman received the cultural blessing. Just as one presents a gift to the bride and groom when they become one, so God gave a wedding gift to his imagebearers, male and female. He gave them the earth, unpolluted, blemish-free, verdant, and fertile. And he called them to give tender, loving care to his creatures and creation. Together male and female were called to be parents. Together they were assigned productive stewardship.

Creation—Again?

Genesis 2:18–25

Now, perhaps, the puzzling part. This passage presents the creation of man and woman as *two distinct* acts of God. Just one chapter earlier the author described creation as a *single* act. It's the kind of puzzle that makes nonbelievers ask: "How can you believe that God created human beings when you see a contradiction like this one and others?"

We Christians don't get too upset about such questions because we're quite willing to admit that we don't completely understand the mystery of God or his Word. At the same time we must also admit that we don't always agree about how to deal with such contrasting narratives. Some of us accept the message of Genesis 1 while ignoring the implications of Genesis 2. Others insist on accepting Genesis 2 while disregarding Genesis 1. Both positions have their shortcomings. The fallacy lies in thinking that because these passages are apparently incongruous, they are incompatible. Not so; we must continue seeking enriching, truthful, relevant interpretations, using the best scholarship available, sound hermeneutic principles, and a prayerful approach.

Head and Helper

The account of God's creation of man and woman as two distinct acts is challenging to some, annoying to others. Most of the problems revolve around the concept of headship: do the passages indicate that one human being is above the other?

Many answer yes. Genesis 2, they say, teaches that women are inferior. Such people might agree with Martin Luther, who said, "Men have broad and large chests, and small narrow hips, and more understanding than women, who have but small and narrow chests, and broad hips, to the end they should bear and bring up children" (*Table Talk,* DCCXXV, 1569).

Others disagree. In the garden, they point out, Adam and Eve ate the same food, drank the same water, lived the same life together. God did not merely fashion a clay figure and bake it in an oven, as a myth suggests. Nor was he building a robot from a single bone into which he breathed life. The entire creative act is shrouded in breathtaking mystery. Woman is not an object, a lesser partner; she is synonymous, one with man's own self—even though chronologically and biologically man has priority. Because Adam was created first doesn't make man superior to woman; animals, after all, are not considered superior to man because they were created before man.

Who *is* the head? Although the word *head* doesn't appear until Genesis 3, it is generally agreed that in Genesis 2 (and elsewhere) the Bible teaches the headship of man in marriage. And as Christians we must honor what God has ordained. In a society where one out of every two marriages ends in divorce, where little children are confused and hurt by the resulting turmoil, and where many households do not have a male head, we see vividly that God's ordinances cannot be ignored with impunity.

Thus, in all of its statements, the church has sought to honor and promote stable Christian marriage and family. No matter which roles women or men fill in the life of the church and of the community, such roles may not be to the hurt of healthy marriage and family relationships.

For that reason we must be as clear as possible about the biblical meaning of *headship.* And although Genesis 2 doesn't explicitly use the word *headship*, some persons feel there *is a clear reference to it in this passage. "To be noted is the fact that man, upon seeing the woman, gives her a name. To give a name to a person—and this is certainly true in oriental society—is to exercise a degree of authority over that person"* (*Acts of Synod 1978,* p. 505).

Is this inference valid? To accept illustrations of customs and rituals as expressive of the sociological climate of a particular nation *is* legitimate. In fact, we need such background to interpret God's Word for our own culture and time. But we must be careful in drawing parallels to verify that we are making a valid inference about a text.

The concept of *headship,* which may be defined as "the position, office, or dignity of a head," brings with it a certain authority, responsibility, or accountability for the direction or course of a marriage. This authority, of course, is to be exercised in loving service. For Christians, the supreme metaphor is the headship of Christ over his body, the church.

A *helper,* on the other hand, is a person who helps, aids, or assists. The connotation of the word suggests that the helper is a little less than the person being helped. He or she has less authority, less skill, less strength, or even less ability. So when woman is considered the helper in a relationship, it becomes very difficult for many people to think of man and woman as equals.

Marriage, it must be remembered, is a very special relationship, magnificently designed by God and badly distorted by human beings. The significance of this special relationship is that it is the consequence of Almighty God looking down on lonely man, the prince of God's creative act, and seeing (Gen. 2:18) that it was not good for man to be alone. So God created "a helper fit for him." Thus the biblical ideas of head and helper go hand-in-hand. Headship here is beautiful; it is part of the mystique of a relationship where two persons become one and where each partner, in love, submits to the other (Eph. 5:21–23). Helping, in such a relationship, is the function of *both* partners—not just the wife.

Still, another implication should be considered: does the word *helper* necessarily imply male headship? This question begs for an answer. Why differing positions remain can be seen by looking at two viewpoints.

Genesis 2:24 talks about man leaving his parents to "cleave to his wife" and with her "become one flesh." This suggests that the entire passage focuses precisely on the marital relationship, not on other life relationships.

But Genesis 2:18–23 shows "an affinity and attraction present between humans that is not present" between "persons and animals." Marriage builds up that affinity of humankind for each other. Thus some people contend that this suggests that Genesis 2 is speaking about man–woman relationships in addition to a marital relationship (*Acts*, 1978, p. 505).

Heads and Bosses

When there are two people in a relationship other than marriage—relationships such as employer–employee, president–vice president, or sergeant–corporal—and the word *helper* (see Gen. 2:18) is used, it may imply that one member of the pair is the head, the other is the hand. The question is whether male headship, as seen in divinely instituted marriage, also holds in the same way in all other life relationships. If it holds in *all* spheres, women must forever be junior partners.

The best translation for *helper* in this Genesis story is "partner" (*Acts*, 1973, p. 521). Helper, or partner, should be understood here in terms of parity. Dr. Clarence Vos (*Women in Old Testament Worship*, p. 16) explains that sometimes the translation *helper* is "understood as though it meant a helper in the sense of a subordinate assistant." But helper is also used to refer to God. In Psalm 46:1 God is "a very present help in trouble." Fifteen references to God as helper can be found in the Old Testament. One could hardly assume from this that God is the subordinate and that the man whom God helps is the head!

Augustine's explanation seems more likely to fit the general man–woman relationship:

> If God meant woman to be superior to man, he would have created her from man's head; or if he wanted her to be inferior to man, he would have made her from his feet. Her creation from man's side shows her to be of equal value; she is to stand side by side to him in all of life.

It's important that we decide which understanding

of *headship* is correct. Why? Because the interpretation reaches into the doctrinal beliefs and statements of the Christian Reformed Church. In questions relating to both structure and function, for example, within the framework of "sphere sovereignty," how are humanly designed offices to work? In practical terms may a woman serve as school principal if there are men on the faculty? Can a woman serve as president of a company if men occupy positions lower in the hierarchy? May a woman be a Supreme Court judge and exercise authority over the lives of literally thousands of men? May Margaret Thatcher be England's prime minister?

And what about the widow and the unmarried woman? If the male headship principle is not limited to marriage relationships, will the widow and unmarried woman be "headless"? Whom will they "help" if they have no husband?

Paul and Headship

1 Corinthians 11:2–16

The story of creation is not limited to Genesis. Thousands of years later another writer, the apostle Paul, echoes creation's greatness and its ramifications throughout the Bible, demonstrating the organic unity of promise and fulfillment running from Old Testament into New Testament. Often he reached back to laws, concepts, and principles established in the Old Testament.

Paul needs no introduction. He is the New Testament rebel turned servant, the persecutor turned defender, the traditionalist turned liberator. Yet readers get confused by some of his masterful rhetoric, particularly as it seems to militate against women being and becoming full partners with men in the body of Christ, the church militant.

Actually, Paul was not a male chauvinist, as many charge. He saw only saved sinners who had to stop dead in their traditional tracks, stop long enough to grasp, fully and thankfully, that the old chains of Jewish legalism had been torn off. Believers were free! Not only free from keeping the law as a way of salvation, but free to keep the law as a rule for thankful Christian living. Free to go forward in faith. Free to worship God. Free to serve him and their fellows.

They only had to learn how. Freedom in Christ did not

come naturally in that day, anymore than it does for the new Christian today. Paul's contemporaries had to learn to live freely to God's glory. Paul had to teach them that Jews couldn't expect Gentile converts to follow Jewish traditions anymore than Christian Reformed folk can insist that new Christians observe the same Sunday evening socialization get-togethers that they enjoy. He had to teach them about meat and idols, about tongues and gifts, and about their need for each other.

In the eleventh chapter of his first letter, Paul talks to the Corinthian church about the proper conduct of women in church. He refers to the Genesis account of the priority of man–husband in relationship to woman–wife within the order of creation in making his pronouncements.

This passage focuses on women wearing veils during worship. One might well wonder why the absence or presence of a veil was such a big issue that it had to be included in the Bible. Its symbolic meaning and association must surely have been highly significant. It certainly is more than a matter of fashion, much more than a matter of twentieth-century women wearing slacks to church (or men attending church tieless and without coats).

It's more like the clothing issue in the late 1960s and early 70s. In an attempt to speak against the values of the establishment, young men and women at that time attended church in shabby jeans, work shirts, tattered and even soiled clothing. Although they succeeded in shocking many people, their message was frequently lost. Why? Because in violating tradition so dramatically, they lost their audience. People were often so repelled that they didn't and couldn't hear.

That's the same kind of problem Paul was addressing. Women who flouted the propriety of wearing veils shocked the church. Only women of ill-repute appeared in public unveiled. Can't you imagine the skepticism, the alarm, the disdain even, that must have greeted those veilless women in Paul's day? Even though James (2:2–4) did not think that the fineness of one's clothing should make any difference in the church, Paul sensed an issue far deeper than externalities; he saw a violation of custom so deep-rooted and freighted with meaning it would offend not only the church itself but also mar its witness to the community outside. The infant church was in too precarious a position to allow such scorning of good order.

Paul, it should be noted, was dealing with many questions. If you read all the chapters from 1 Corinthians 7 through 1 Corinthians 14, you will find that Paul chides the church for several practices. The Christians he addresses were not accustomed to handling properly their precious freedom, newly found in Christ. They carried freedom too far; they didn't differentiate adequately between liberty and license (see 1 Cor. 10:23).

Of course, Paul is not talking merely of fashion standards; in fact, he is not referring to any cultural principle. He is stating a principle and applying it to a cultural situation of his day. It was as disgraceful for a woman to pray and prophesy with her head uncovered as it was for a man to do so with his head covered. At issue is a principle, a principle of relationships.

What Paul says seems clear. Yet the principles of hermeneutics (see Appendix C) don't permit us to stop and accept the *apparent* meaning without careful analysis. Several statements which have been made about this passage should be carefully considered and evaluated.

> *Because this passage refers to the creation order, the statement Paul makes about veils, long hair, and shaved heads is a universal and abiding principle which applies for all times and all places.*

Paul bases his pronouncement on God's work of creating man first and woman out of man. But are the first human beings man and woman generally or are they husband and wife only? The Greek words *aner* for husband and *gunu* for wife may also be translated as man and woman. (See especially verses 3, 8, and 9.) Since Paul's words are based on creation, the command sounds like a permanent norm. Why, we must ask then, is this norm so blatantly disregarded today, not only in secular society but also among Christians? (If women today return to the custom of wearing veils, it will not be because Paul has said so but because Madison Avenue so prescribes. And if wearing veils is a permanent norm, then women must repent for not wearing veils and the "heads" must repent for having allowed the women to sin.)

This is only a specific application of a general rule for right conduct in worship.

If this is an *application* of a principle rather than the principle itself, the Bible reader needs to uncover or discover what that principle is.

As we reflect on this, it might be well to think of an average Sunday morning worship service in the Christian Reformed Church. Why, for example, are asterisks put on the printed liturgy to indicate when to stand? Why are we asked, after the benediction, to stand quietly until the organist begins to play? Why is the entire liturgy planned carefully and principially? Why have many churches introduced nurseries and children's worship? The Christian Reformed Church prides itself (and rightly so) on its orderly and meaningful worship services. We have principles which undergird our actions and conduct. Maybe Paul needed to show the church of his day what it means to "worship God in Spirit and truth." It had yet to learn that all things are to be done decently and in good order.

Given this context, it seems appropriate to recognize that the abiding principle here is reverence in worship. With this principle in mind, the reader must decide whether the limitations Paul mentions should or do apply to women's roles in the church of the twentieth century.

Paul is giving us contradictory instructions. First he speaks of man's priority in creation (vv. 8 and 9); then he speaks of man's dependence on women (vv. 11 and 12) in the ongoing development of creation.

This may seem like a contradiction, but actually it helps direct us to a basic question: can either man or woman continue alone? Shouldn't we acknowledge that man and woman stand in a mutual relationship of dependence to each other and in a mutual submission to God—"for all things are from God" (v. 12)?

We've been looking, in this chapter, at some difficult parts of Scripture. These have very immediate bearing on the question of whether or not women should use their God-given gifts in the various offices of the church. In studying and discussing these passages we should keep clearly in mind, first, that all of these are chapters and verses from God's Word, written under the guidance of God's Spirit, and, second, that these are parts of a whole, of the "big picture" given us in the Bible. If we keep this in mind, these and other "problematic" texts bearing on this issue (1 Cor. 14 and 1 Tim. 2, discussed in chapter 7), may become less a source of disagreement and more a basis on which we come to a solution of the issue.

Study
Session

First

As a basis for our discussion of chapter 4, read and reflect on the creation accounts in Genesis 1:26–31 and Genesis 2:15–24. Discuss briefly how group members personally handle the apparent contradictions between Genesis 1 and Genesis 2. Are the accounts incompatible?

Second

Chapter 4 discusses the essence of the problem of women in office: *headship*. Many of the discussion questions which follow focus on the implications of that term.

1. What are the dangers of not keeping the panoramic view of Scripture in mind while studying the issue of men and women as partners in the church?

2. Most of us would agree that Christians ought to work toward the restoration of God's kingdom until such time as it is consummated (Stage Four). But how do we relate the problem of women in office to this? Should we maintain the status quo until Stage Four, or should we work toward restoring women to Christian service now? Explain.

3. Practically speaking, how does headship express itself in your family? Do you see any suggestions here for the church?

4. How do *you* interpret Paul's teaching (1 Cor. 11) about

the necessity of women wearing veils? Do you regard this as a universal principle? If so, why do Christians so blatantly disregard it today? Or do you regard this veil commandment as an application of the broader principle of reverence in worship, as explained in chapter 4? What are the implications of your choice for the issue of the role of women in the church?

5. Should what Paul says about the limited role of women in worship be extended to all or none of the other spheres of society (i.e., schools, government, business, media, etc.). Consider the implications, especially in view of the steadily changing position of women in society today.

6. Leaders of institutions for higher Christian education in Zimbabwe, Swaziland, Malawi, and Kenya attended a conference in the United States in the summer of 1981. Women in those countries don't enjoy the equality in civil life that North American women do. Yet, in the churches in these lands women hold office because, the representatives said, freedom in Christ applies to all. How do you explain this curious difference between the Christian Reformed Church and these African churches?

Third

Don't be disappointed if your group has had more than a little disagreement today. Remember, we are dealing with the heart of the issue, and it would be unreasonable to expect basic conflicts to be suddenly resolved. On the other hand, some progress, some new insights may have been gained. Take a moment to allow each group member an opportunity to share any new insights, any change in perspective, which chapter 4 and/or today's discussion may have brought out.

Fourth

A concluding prayer:

Father, God, Creator,
who laid the earth's foundations,

shut up the seas behind doors,
made storehouses for snow and hail.

Who disperses the lightning,
and gives birth to the frost.

We stand humbly
in our creatureliness,
yet ask your acceptance
of our praise for your works
on earth, in sky, and sea,
and your creation
of man,
of woman.

Help us to fathom
the greatness of principles
established by your decree,
for our well-being.

In the name of Christ,
Amen.

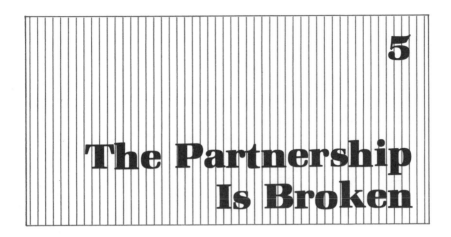

The Partnership Is Broken

Looking at life from a twentieth-century vantage point, one might say Adam and Eve had it made: a marriage literally "made in heaven," perfect health, full employment, no budgeting or inflation, no pollution or poverty, no threat of nuclear annihilation, and—best of all—a flawless relationship with God. How tragic that they didn't keep it that way. Their idyllic lifestyle was soon bedeviled.

The Fall

"It was that wily snake, you know."

"It was that woman, you know."

But God said sternly, "No excuses!"

Once it was introduced, sin affected all people, men and women, for all time with its awful corruption. Both the man and the woman were responsible; both were addressed by God; both responded to God; both tried excuses. So unified were they that a parity existed between them even in their evil.

The consequences of the fall into sin came equally yet differently to both. The unique agony of birth pangs was allotted to the woman. In addition, the perfect marital relationship between them was replaced by her husband's "rule." Harsh toil was assigned to the man. The ground would yield weeds; blights and insects would damage plants; storms and droughts would plague the crops. Honest work would become hard drudgery. He and his family would eat only after hot and sweaty labor.

The ruin and corruption was devastatingly complete; no one and no thing was exempt. Male and female have since lived with the results of God's early frown. They soon discovered each other's flaws, deficiencies, and sins. Things were no longer the same between them. What remained was only a shadowy caricature of the original God-given relationship.

Men and women throughout the world still experience the pains, troubles, and disharmony that came with the fall. They work hard to counteract those distortions, to alleviate or minimize the pain of childbirth and the misery of labor, to heal the relationship of husband and wife. But the suffering remains.

Christian men and women are people who have been forgiven and liberated in Christ from sin's bonds. They are restored, redeemed, and free. But—and here is a vital question bearing on this issue—does this restoration in Christ include a liberation from all the consequences of the fall, even the "desire" and "rule" of the curse? Was that curse in Genesis 3 a prescription of what man–woman relationships ought to be after the fall or was it a description of the corruption from which they should be redeemed?

The answer to this question has immense implications for the partnership of men and women and for their equal and cooperative tasks within the church and the Christian community.

To some Christian thinkers the fall into sin forever precludes women from holding any church office. Tertullian, one of the early church fathers, called woman the "devil's gateway." After all, she was created last and fell into sin first. So she must be weaker.

On the other hand, it seems reasonable to conclude that if Adam were stronger he wouldn't have listened to Eve. God didn't blame Eve for the sin of the whole race—that seems to fall on Adam. As 1 Corinthians 15:22 says, "For as in Adam all die, so also in Christ shall all be made alive." And the argument of some that Eve was deceived because she was *naturally* weaker is hard to defend from what the Bible has said about the goodness of God's creation.

John Calvin also speaks to the issue, arguing that since a woman had "seduced man from God's commandment" it was appropriate that she be "deprived of all her freedom and placed under the yoke." He bases his opinion on 1 Timothy 2:14 where Paul says, "[It] was the woman [who] was deceived and became a transgressor." But as Paul points out, the woman was deceived while the man sinned with his eyes open. God had directly commanded Adam not to eat the fruit of that particular tree (Gen. 2:16–17).

Satan's cunning cannot be overlooked. He attacked the human race at its very core—the man–woman relationship. This suggests the deeply rooted importance of this relationship as the genetic origin and starting point for the unfolding of other life relationships. The corruption was radical, ugly, sweeping. We only have to look at today's divorces, at single-head families, and at children confused by a half-dozen sets of grandparents or by two dads or moms to know the octopus character of harmful and hurting relationships. Divide and conquer and thus destroy was Satan's strategy then and it's still his strategy today.

It was part of woman's curse that not only her union but also her parity with man became undone; it was in the context of this curse that her husband's headship became a rule of dominion. Male leadership makes way for male domination, and female subjection results in limited (or unlimited) surrender. Subsequent biblical and social history shows how this sin-plagued authority was exercised and often abused.

One curious aspect of this awful story is that though Adam is held accountable for sin in humankind, God addresses Eve when he points out how salvation and redemption will be achieved. From the "seed" of woman will come the Redeemer who will crush the serpent's head (Gen. 3:15). Woman is assigned a major and central role here. God's promise to Eve increased the joy of motherhood. Jewish girls dreamed about becoming the mother of the coming Messiah. Many centuries elapsed before Jesus actually came, but during that Old Testament era the hints of future renewal appeared like morning stars pointing to the dawn of the new day.

Hints of Light

The Old Testament picture of the life of men and women shows the continuing effects of the fall. The curse of sin is woven into the fabric of social relationships.

Man must earn bread by the sweat of his brow. It is not work that is his punishment but the harsh uncertainties of life. The early Israelites were nomadic shepherds and stock-breeders, searching often for water, fending off robbers and predators, keeping watch over their livestock by day and night. And later Israelites were also farmers and field-hands, digging and plowing, planting and harvesting. They labored long and hard.

Woman's lot wasn't any better; in fact, it was often far worse. A young girl was declared ready for marriage as soon as she could bear a child. She called her husband "Lord" and "Master." His wish and word served as her command.

Women received no education even long after education opportunities were available for men. They legally belonged first to their fathers and then to their husbands. They had no legal rights themselves. Women stood while men ate. They covered their faces with veils whenever they walked outdoors. Israelite law considered women irresponsible and weak.

Still, because they were weak, the Mosaic law also protected them. Compared to the cultures of the Canaanites and surrounding pagan societies, an Israelite woman was honored and respected, especially in her role as mother. Children were required by God's commandment to honor their parents. A woman's husband also honored her; in fact, he often placed her on a pedestal.

The problem was that a woman had to stay on the pedestal. If she fell off, judgment was hard. Whatever "ruling" she did, she had to do surreptitiously. Remember how Sarah convinced Abraham to sleep with Hagar and how Rebekah deceived Isaac by having Jacob, incognito, secure Esau's blessing? They were manipulative.

The laws of Moses also showed a disparity between men and women in Israel. The woman owed her husband total fidelity, but not vice versa. Men could seek divorce; women could not. Men, on the other hand, were legally obligated to maintain their wives. Disparity between men and women was further demonstrated in the public arena with the restriction that all civic and religious leaders in Israel had to be males. The messianic hope, the bright and morning star, was also to be a male.

Looking for the hints of light through all this is like taking a minicourse in Old Testament history. Sarah isn't just a mother who gains respect and recognition because of the fifth commandment of the law. She is a *covenant* mother. Even though Rebekah deceived Isaac, she also made a choice which reflected trust in God's promise. Ruth joined the lineage of Christ. Hannah gave her little one to God. Women were important, yet generally their role was limited to the task of motherhood.

But some women did play other significant roles in the life of the covenant community. Miriam (Ex. 5; Num. 12; Mic. 6: 3–4) was a coleader with Aaron. She played a major role in celebrating God's victory for Israel at the exodus. Deborah (Judg. 4 and 5) by default became the leader of God's people in a time of crisis. She played both a prophetic and kingly role during one of Israel's periods of apostasy. Huldah (2 Kings 22; 2 Chron. 34) is not mentioned often, but many consulted her. "Thus saith the Lord," she said to Israel's leaders, using the same language we associate with our ministers today. She spoke authoritatively to males in authority, both priests and kings.

Some say these are exceptions which prove nothing. Just because some women rose above male authority in particular circumstances doesn't prove there should be women in established offices. They maintain that, while women did play a large and noteworthy role in Israel's history, it is clear that generally speaking very few Old Testament women held office. *Office* here is defined as "a divinely instituted position, one in which people served from generation to generation, and in which the officeholder was a representative between God and his people."

Perhaps exceptions are best used neither to prove nor disprove a point. The women who served in exceptional ways and positions in the Old Testament should be looked upon as morning stars, faintly heralding a coming brighter day when the Light of the world would make it possible for women to serve more completely and fully.

Between the Testaments

In the final centuries just before the long promised redemption came, no Bible books were written. But the fourteen Apocryphal books and other Jewish writings appeared during the centuries following the return from exile. During this period most of the Jews lived in foreign lands. In God's providence they affected the thought patterns of other nations but were also influenced by these cultures.

Women in that era generally continued to hold a lesser place in society. In Greco–Roman culture, for example, female inferiority was the rule. Women stayed home; they led—and were expected to lead—secluded, submissive lives. So it isn't surprising that during this time in Israel too the role of women seemed to hit a low point.

But the Old Testament era was coming to a close. Soon, through the seed of the woman, God would remove the sorrow of the curse and replace it with redemption and reconciliation for all, male and female, who believe in him.

Study Session

First

This chapter discusses the consequences of the fall on the male–female and husband–wife relationships. But along with this devastating historical event the veiled beginnings of promised restoration also emerge. To capture this sad yet promising story, read Genesis 3:8–19 and Joel 2:21–29 for your opening devotions.

It is reassuring for Christians to know that as early as the third chapter of the first book of the Bible a way out is promised—the way of the cross. Considering the original perfect creation, the devastation of the fall, and the restoration through redemption, the predominant issue for our discussion today is whether the fall into sin forever precludes women from holding office in the church.

Second

Select from among the following discussion questions:

1. Would you agree that the kinds of roles women played in the Old Testament gradually increased in significance, moving from single instances of women filling typically masculine roles to Joel's prophecy of the Spirit filling sons *and* daughters, male *and* female servants? Does the Old Testament thereby prepare the way for the restoration of the male–female relationship? In answering these questions, look more closely

at the various *kinds* of roles women held in the Old Testament.

2. You may have heard it said that there's much work for women to do in the church and that it's only their desire for status that is creating the current debate over women in office. What do you think? Is the issue one of women's rights more than it is an issue of serving God fully? You may wish to compare the two viewpoints.

3. On the basis of Genesis 3, do you agree that the rule of men/husbands over women/wives as decreed by God is part of the universal curse following our human fall into sin?

4. Look at the *curses* sin brought upon the human race. What attempts are made to overcome these curses in work? In nature? In childbirth? What attempts have been made to overcome the dominance of men over women?

5. Miriam participated in a rebellion against Moses (Num. 12). Later in the Bible she gets an honorable mention (Mic. 6:4). Do you consider her a positive or negative example in the issue being studied? Why?

6. It has been said that a Jewish boy's prayer was: "Lord, I thank thee for not making me a Gentile, or a slave, or a woman." Do you see any possible connection between this and Galatians 3:28?

7. How did a Hebrew woman find her identity? How does this differ from women today? Should women today find their identity in the same fashion as Old Testament women did?

8. During Old Testament times divorce was usually advantageous for men but not for women (Deut. 24:1–4). Why did God allow this? (See Matt. 19:3–8.)

9. Does the replacement of circumcision with baptism have any bearing on the issue of women in church office? Explain.

10. Some have been quick to blame Christianity and its related traditions for the lower status of women in Western culture. How valid is this judgment? Does the

denial of women holding office in the church have any relevance to this discussion? Explain.

By way of a summary of your class discussion, comment on this observation: "No far-reaching conclusions should be drawn from the data and examples taken from the Old Testament."

Third

Here is a prayer which you may use to conclude the session:

Our Father,
you are dear
as Father–Mother,
and so much more.
We are your children,
sons–daughters,
and more.
We are servants,
frail and weak,
dependent on promises
kept by your Son,
our Lord,
on the cross.
Teach us crystal,
where we are dull.
Teach us warm,
where we are cold.
So we, your children,
your daughters–sons,
may, in you,
be one and won.
Amen.

The Witness of the Gospel

Four hundred years had gone by since the close of the Old Testament period. The Jews were now a subjugated people, part of the vast Roman Empire. Their downfall and diaspora (dispersion) had weakened them politically, but it had strengthened their dream of a Messiah, the One who would throw off the heavy yoke of the Romans and once again establish a glorious Jewish kingdom.

Though many peoples had converged on Israel, the main influences affecting them came from the dominant Greco–Roman culture. These included the ideas which these societies held about women. Whereas the Romans generally did not extend education to women, the Greeks were more open to this. Many Greek women received education up to the secondary level, and there were even some female professors. On the other hand, while the Greeks provided more educational opportunities for women, the Romans integrated women more fully into their society.

Still, then as now, there was a clear double standard for male and female. Married women began to receive some rights in society, but this—then as now—frightened many people into predicting that female freedom would lead to a breakdown in family life. (Family breakdown does exist today, but it's due to many complex factors and shouldn't be blamed simplistically on the changing role of women alone.)

The assimilation of various ideas from the cultures of the Greeks and Romans had at some points modified current Jewish traditions, but it hadn't changed the status of women very much. Most Jewish men still considered women irresponsible and not worth educating. They described females as garrulous, greedy, idle, jealous, vain, voluptuous, and forward. Blessed indeed was the Hebrew man who had a good wife. The rabbis and rulers of Israel were not about to relax the prevalent restrictions placed on their women.

It is in this cultural context that Jesus' attitudes and actions toward women should be viewed. It is in contrast to these general opinions that we can begin to understand how Jesus' approach to women puzzled and greatly provoked the ecclesiastical establishment.

Jesus and the Old Testament Tradition

Nobody in history has ever done so much for women as has Jesus Christ.

Jesus was a Jew. In many ways he was not conspicuously different from other Jewish men. He spoke Aramaic with some Greek phrases. He knew his Scriptures. (At the age of twelve his questions about these Old Testament writings baffled and dumbfounded the church leaders.) He didn't come forward with a lot of new ideas but rather with richer and truer interpretations of God's Word. Jesus was very Jewish; which, of course, makes his elevation of women so beautiful.

Jesus was a radical—his attitude toward women was a radical departure from the customs and practices of his day—but not a social revolutionary. He was heir to all that was purest in Jewish thought. He brought out the true implications of the rabbis' own tradition coming up out of the Old Testament.

Some have supposed that Jesus rejected and condemned all observance of the Mosaic law. That is not so. Rather, he taught the truer meaning of law over against distortions of it. Concerning himself and the law, Jesus said:

"Think not that I have come to abolish the law and the prophets; I have come not to abolish them but to fulfill them. For truly, I say to you, till heaven and earth pass away, not an iota, not a dot, will pass from the law until all is accomplished. Whoever then relaxes one of the least of these commandments and teaches men so, shall be called least in the kingdom of heaven . . ." (Matt. 5:17–19a).

Jesus Christ did not supersede the law; he fulfilled it. Reversing the word *fulfill* to *fill-full* gives a more visual expression of Jesus' attitude toward the law. First, he taught its richness; second, he satisfied God's requirement of perfect obedience to it; third, he taught and showed that love and service are the essence of the law.

Jesus showed a similar fulfilling freedom toward tradition. Tradition to him was important, but only as a guideline. His attitude toward it often shocked the Jews, for Jesus went further than the most openhearted rabbi when he accepted all those who came to him in faith—the uncircumcised pagan, the open sinner, and the unbeliever—as a sister or brother. Particularly shocking to most of the Jewish leaders was Jesus' attitude and behavior toward women. He repeatedly broke the bounds of pharisaic law in this area; Jesus strove to restore and renew the original divinely ordained partnership of men and women as coworkers in the heavenly kingdom.

Jesus and Women

Women played an important role in Jesus' life. Every Christian knows about Mary and Elizabeth and their relationship to the Savior at the beginning of his life. God chose to honor the eighty-four-year-old widow–prophetess, Anna, who never left the temple, worshiping day and night, fasting and praying. By faith Anna saw the redemption of God's people in the infant Jesus.

Jesus also played a great role in the lives of many women. What he did and how he spoke to them astonished these women. To better understand the revolutionary dimensions of Jesus' acts—words and deeds that evoked feelings of anger, bewilderment, shock, amazement, and delight in the crowds that surrounded him—we should try to view them through the eyes of the women they involved.

Consider the dinner incident with Mary and Martha in Luke 10:38–42. Martha complained to Jesus not only because her sister had neglected to work in the kitchen and help prepare the meal but also because she had overstepped the bounds of female modesty by sitting at Jesus' feet, listening to him, and discussing ideas with him.

"Martha, Martha," Jesus said, "You are anxious and troubled

about many things; one thing is needful. Mary has chosen the good portion, which shall not be taken away from her" (vv. 41–42). Imagine both Mary's and Martha's feelings on hearing this message. This was a tremendous step forward for all Jewish women. Disciples, Jesus said in effect, can be either male or female.

Remember the crippled woman (Luke 13:10–17)? For eighteen years she had been unable to stand up straight. Then Jesus came one Sabbath and said, "You are free." The indignant ruler of the synagogue couldn't very well condemn Jesus' healing act, but he complained, "Did it have to be on the sabbath day?" Jesus chided him, saying, "You'd give your donkey water on the Sabbath Day; why shouldn't this daughter of Abraham be set free?" It must have been music to her ears—"daughter of Abraham"—a child of the covenant.

Think of the woman who suffered from a hemorrhage for twelve years (Matt. 9:20–22). What a risk she took in trying to touch Jesus' garment! Not only was she a woman, but she suffered from an embarrassing private problem. Her blood flow made her unclean (Lev. 15:19–30), so she was publicly shunned by everyone who knew of her illness.

This woman inched her way through the crowd and touched the hem of Jesus' garment. "Who touched me?" he asked. (He too was now defiled and unclean under Jewish law.) Fear drowned the joy of healing. She fell at Jesus' feet and told him the truth. He replied compassionately, "Your faith has healed you. You are free." It was *her* faith, not that of her husband (through whom Jewish women traditionally found religious identity), that brought healing and redemption.

As a last example, there is the story of the Samaritan woman (John 4:1–42). Women's status was low in Israel, but a Samaritan woman was beneath the lowest. It could hardly be imagined that a Jew would speak to a Samaritan man, let alone a Samaritan woman.

Yet Jesus conversed long and earnestly with this woman, accepted water from her, and showed her the way of salvation, the path of real freedom. Upon returning from the city, the disciples were dumbfounded when they saw Jesus talking with this Samaritan woman. Jesus said to them, "Come. Now is the harvest time. Some have sown and have worked the ground. You are to reap the harvest."

For centuries the gospel seed had been planted and now Jesus, the promised One, had come to finish the Father's work. It was a cause for celebration! And this Samaritan woman, with a questionable relationship to the covenant (she claimed Jacob as her father), was included by Jesus. Her excitement was obvious.

Jesus' pure and gracious conduct toward women must have invited gazes of scorn, dumbfounded looks of surprise and curiosity, and bitter mutterings, expressing the fear that women wouldn't be easy to live with after all that attention. But Jesus' mission was also to women. He came to free them from sin and its results, from their centuries-old cultural chains, and from the distorted view of the man–woman and husband–wife partnerships. Jesus was a friend to women. He treated them as whole human beings, as much in need of grace and redemption as men.

And women publicly returned that attention. Mary of Bethany poured perfume on his feet and dried them with her hair (John 12:1–3). The woman at the Pharisee's house did much the same thing (Luke 7:36–38). Women followed Jesus to the cross. They assisted him whenever and however they could.

Jesus' Teachings for Women

The Bible shows us that Jesus used forms of teaching to which women could relate. Some of his parables use metaphors taken out of the woman's everyday life:

    —The ten virgins (Matt. 25:1–13)
    —The lamp on a stand (Mark 4:21–23)
    —The yeast in the dough (Luke 13:20–21)
    —The lost coin (Luke 15:8–10)
    —The persistent widow (Luke 18:1–8)

Furthermore, as one Bible scholar has pointed out, there is a "complementary parallelism in Luke's relating of the gospel story that demonstrates how Jesus chose both male and female to illustrate his teachings" (Helmut Flender, *St. Luke, Theologian of Redemption History,* quoted in *Acts,* 1973, p. 542). Consider the following:

    —The angelic annuniciation to Zechariah and Mary (Luke 1:11–20, 26–38)

—Simeon and Anna (Luke 2:25–38)

—The healing of the demoniac and Peter's mother-in-law (Luke 4:31–39; cf. Mark 1:21–31)

—The faith of the centurion of Capernaum and the widow of Nain (Luke 7:1–17)

—Simon the Pharisee and the woman who was a sinner (Luke 7:36–50)

—The good samaritan and Mary and Martha (Luke 10:29–42)

—The parables of the man with a mustard seed and the woman with leaven (Luke 13:18–21)

—The parable of the man with a hundred sheep and the woman with ten pieces of silver (Luke 15:3–10)

—The women at the tomb and the disciples going to Emmaus (Luke 23:44–24:35)

The corrective character of Jesus' teaching is well illustrated by the story in John 8:1–11. A woman was "caught in adultery." Obviously she was not alone, and according to Leviticus 20:10, both the man and the woman caught were to be put to death. The Jewish leaders brought only the woman to Jesus. When they asked him what to do, Jesus said, "Let him who is without sin among you be the first to throw a stone at her." One by one the crowd slunk away. To the woman Jesus said, "Neither do I condemn you; go and do not sin again." Thus, quite effectively, Jesus demolished the double standard.

Summary

In Jesus' actions and words we see a breakthrough from the second-rate position of Jewish women. Men and women, in Christ's eyes, were on equal footing—both were sinners in need of redemption and both were graciously and completely redeemed if they believed in him.

Still the undeniable fact remains that Jesus didn't choose any women to be included with his twelve apostles. This is evidence, some have pointed out, that although Jesus brought freedom and equality for women, he nowhere appointed them to special offices.

While it is certainly true that the office of apostle was filled only by men, this does not suggest that to Jesus women were not equal with men. He clearly affirmed their worth, testifying that male and female, man and woman, are alike and equal in God's eyes. A human parallel to this can be seen in the equality of children in relationship to their parents. Which child would you give up if you had to give up one? Or, to use a different parallel, which part of the body would you relinquish first—the eye, the ear, the tongue? Aren't they of equal value to us?

Some have argued that such equality means that people should be assigned to office according to gifts, not according to sex. Yet equality does not *necessarily* mean sameness in function. Rather, functions should vary according to the gifts God has given. If one takes these gifts seriously, should discrimination because of sex be abolished? This is the debated point.

What isn't debatable among Christians is that Jesus, the God–man, appeared in history to redeem human beings, men and women, from the chains of sin. He brought total, but not yet completed, redemption and freedom.

Total yet incomplete redemption may seem contradictory, but it isn't. During World War II anxiously waiting wives and parents and fellow citizens rejoiced on D-day, June 6, 1944. Thousands of allied soldiers had landed in Normandy. Casualties were heavy, yet rejoicing prevailed. For all practical purposes, the war had been won. That decisive landing in Normandy meant victory for the allies. Only the mopping-up assignment needed to be completed—and that took another fifteen months.

So also Christ on the cross won total and permanent victory over sin and Satan. His followers are now called to engage in the mopping-up operations, continuing to work for the advancement and completion of his established kingdom, preparing for the time when Jesus Christ himself will come to claim it.

None of us questions that Jesus came for both men and women. But some do question if his redemption also includes freedom and equality for women. Yet one dimension of his mission was the restoration and renewal of the original divinely ordained partnership of men and women as co-workers for God. Jesus took this giant step forward in that history. In a sense, because women had additional bonds to be broken, it may be said that Jesus' life was the biggest turning point in the history of women.

It is in the context of this understanding of the coming, development, and working out of God's kingdom on earth that we, as Christians, should seek to settle the issue of women in office in the Christian Reformed Church.

Study Session

First

This chapter argues that Jesus did much to free women and to give them a place of dignity equal to that of men. You might want to read one or more of the Scripture passages mentioned in chapter 6 that detail Christ's role in the lives of women.

Second

Choose from among the following discussion questions:

1. Is it difficult to understand the negative attitude of the Jewish leaders toward women? Why or why not?

2. Pick one (or more) of the Scripture passages dealt with in chapter 6 and discuss what can be learned from Jesus' actions—for women as well as for men.

3. If Jesus were to live among us today, for which groups would he seek equality? What do you think he would say to the church about the role of women?

4. How do you account for the fact that Jesus didn't appoint women as apostles? Is it valid to argue that since Jesus didn't appoint women to special offices that the church today ought to be content with the remarkable progress he did make? Why or why not?

Third

Sometimes we need to look closely at the cultural context of the Bible. It is especially interesting to compare the styles and customs and mores of biblical times with our own. Doing so may increase our appreciation of the radical character of Christ's ministry.

Was this your experience as you studied and discussed chapter 6? Perhaps you'd be willing to mention a new idea or insight you gained from this chapter or from the discussion today, something you feel may help you toward a resolution of the issue being studied.

Fourth

A concluding prayer:*

Father in heaven,
I praise you,
for I am fearfully, wonderfully made.
Before I was born
your eyes saw my body.
You have searched,
you know me.
You know all my ways.
I praise you, Father.
Your thoughts are precious to me.
You often hem me in,
behind and before,
but your hand is always on me.
I praise you, Father.
Search me, my God.
Test me,
and know my anxiety.
See, O God, if I am offensive
to your children, and
lead me
in the way everlasting.
For Jesus' sake.
Amen.

---

*Thoughts and phrases are from Psalm 139.

Interpreting Apostle Paul

We have seen how Jesus, while not breaking any laws, did set aside certain cultural taboos relating to the subordination of Jewish women. Taboos usually develop for the welfare of society. Often, however, they come to have the force of law. So it was no small matter that Jesus dignified women as God's imagebearers, equal with men.

But the apostle Paul, some say, was not like Jesus. Some women don't like Paul; they consider him a male chauvinist. Such women are wrong, however—wrong in their attitude towards Paul and wrong in their judgment of him.

Paul was the scholar, missionary, and preacher who, with singleness of purpose and without stint, devoted his life to declaring the freedom of redemption. Paul was truly a man of God! Could a man who wrote a letter to the Romans expressing his concern for the eternal well-being of humankind have no care and love for half the human race? Hardly. Of the twenty-six people Paul mentioned in his letters as fellow workers, at least nine were women.

Paul preached freedom in Christ and freedom from the law, not because the law had been abolished, but because it had been fulfilled by Christ. This freedom was not limited to the Jewish male. Paul knew and preached that Christ's call to faith and salvation is one, common, single call. There is not one call for men and another call for women. Paul addresses himself to sinners—Jews and Gentiles, males and females, slaves and free people. Everyone, Paul said, needs to know the way of salvation, freedom, and oneness in Jesus Christ.

Does this spiritual equality bring with it equality of office? Some serious students of Paul's letters say yes. Others say no. And that cannot be. What then shall we say?

Neither Male Nor Female

Galatians 3:28

In this text Paul clearly says that in Christ there is oneness and equality—in Christ there is neither male nor female. This teaching is mentioned wherever and whenever people discuss women as equal partners in the Christian community and in church office. One can claim too little for Galatians 3:28; one can also conclude too much from it. In keeping with sound hermeneutical principles, one should read Paul's entire letter to the Galatians to determine the context of this one verse.

In this epistle to the Galatian church, Paul's central concern was to reaffirm the truth of justification by faith alone through the sovereign grace of God. On the basis of this justification, Paul declares, we are free in Christ. No longer are we chained to a law which we cannot carry out. No longer are we bound to traditions that hobble us. No longer are we separated from others by fences that keep us in and others out. Race, sex, and vocation can no longer divide the body of Christ. Paul emphasizes the redeeming work of Christ— how he overcomes the distorting effects of humanity's fatal fall into sin and restores the fundamental unity in human relationships which God had ordered in his good creation.

Considering Galatians 3:28 in the context of that message, we can see that it teaches—on the basis of Christ's redeeming work which justifies and liberates sinners—that all human beings enjoy spiritual unity and equality before God and within the Christian community. Jews and Gentiles, masters and slaves, males and females—all are now one in the service of the Lord. Thus, in accessibility to and appropriation of salvation, *all* are now *one*.

Paul used examples in Galatians 3:28 of three prevalent dominant–submissive relationships. These were healed in Christ. However, this does not negate other real and legitimate diversities. Anarchy would prevail in society if all rank and order among people were repudiated. God ordained a parent–child relationship which cannot be abused with impunity. He ordained a husband–wife relationship for the mutual joy and welfare of the couple and the care of the children. The deterioration of these relationships brings child abuse, single-parent homes, high divorce rates, non-supportive fathers, and even runaway mothers and children.

Indeed, redemption doesn't erase any of the relationships embedded in creation; rather it renews them. It restores what is corrupt to the perfect creation it was meant to be. Grace is not against nature but against the sin which infests it. Therefore, spiritual unity and equal status before God don't lead to an egalitarian notion of democracy or any other notion about the sameness of all human beings. Rather, the distinctions and diversities given with creation remain. Instead the text speaks against all tendencies to discriminate against certain persons (Gentiles, slaves, women) within the church and to reduce them to second-class citizenship in Christ's kingdom.

Galatians 3:28 does not speak, either directly or decisively, about the respective roles of women and men in the church. Therefore, it doesn't seem to answer the question of who is eligible or ineligible for office in the church. Nor does this text speak directly about gifts—who receives them and how they should be used.

However, this text, as part of Paul's message to the Galatians about justification and liberation, does indirectly encourage us to consider whether all the gifts of women should be used to help build the body of Christ to the coming of his kingdom (Eph. 4:1–16). Not to use every talent and every gift that God has entrusted to every person is wasteful. For that God will surely require an accounting from us.

Keep Silent?

1 Corinthians 14:33–36

Paul, writing to the Corinthian church, has just completed that glorious poem on love (1 Cor. 13). Now he turns to the subject of the gifts of prophecy, speaking in tongues, and orderly worship.

Speaking in tongues, Paul said (1 Cor. 14:1–33), is a gift of the Spirit, but it is also unintelligible. To speak in tongues was like speaking into the air (v. 9). When the Corinthian church got together, everybody wanted to talk. It must have been incredibly noisy, almost beyond the imagination of us who follow a printed liturgy, who know precisely when to read or respond in unison, and who, lest we embarrass fellow worshipers, never register an audible "Amen!" or joyous "Hallelujah!" even when the Spirit moves us. But in the Corinthian church each person had a song, a lesson, a revelation, a tongue, or an interpretation and insisted on voicing it (v. 26).

Paul told the Corinthians to stop thinking like children (v. 20). He might well have added, "And stop acting like kindergartners," but he didn't. He merely said, "Give everybody a chance. Take turns. Everyone needs to be instructed and encouraged. And remember, God is not a God of confusion but of peace."

The intent of this passage is clear. Paul cautioned the people against disorderliness and chaotic conduct in the use of spiritual gifts, especially prophetic utterances. God's Word, then as now, must come across in an understandable and constructive way.

It is in this context that Paul addressed the women. If the young Corinthian church in any way resembled the Jewish synagogue, the noise of women seeking immediate answers would be especially disturbing. In Massachusetts the first colonial synagogue still stands. Today men still occupy the choice seats on the main floor, clustered around the ark of the covenant. On a small balcony (with a separate, outdoor entrance) the women and girls sit. A wife cannot nudge her husband and whisper a question. To be heard by her husband she has to call out. The situation might have been similar in the Corinthian church.

Speaking to that kind of situation, Paul says to the Corinthian women, "You must keep silent. You must not speak in church. If you have questions, wait until you get home and ask your husband for answers. Our God is not a God of confusion but of peace." Paul is insisting on a measure of decorum in a seemingly disordered congregation.

Considering this passage and attempting to relate it to what Paul said earlier (1 Cor. 11) on the subject of the proper conduct of women in worship, students of the Bible have come up with basically three approaches to this injunction for women to keep silent in the church (Acts, 1978, pp. 519ff.).

One view is that this passage was inserted by someone other than Paul. In 1 Corinthians 11:5 Paul said women shouldn't prophesy and pray with their heads uncovered. That would seem to approve of women speaking publicly if properly attired and thus contradict what is said in 1 Corinthians 14:34. This interpretation hasn't generally been accepted.

Another viewpoint suggests that the passage intends only to instruct women to do no *public* speaking in church. But again that seems to clash with 1 Corinthians 11:5 where praying and prophesying aloud are clearly permitted.

The third view suggests that Paul's principle interest here is promoting orderliness in the church. He wanted propriety and decorum upheld. People in the Christian Reformed Church can empathize with this. Note the sharp contrast between our style of worship and a Pentecostal church service.

These three possible viewpoints leave us with a number of knotty questions. Is Paul speaking here only of local circumstances? Does he perhaps have in mind only the unruly behavior of some Corinthian church members, especially women? But Paul says specifically that women should keep silent in the church*es* (plural). If this is true, should women today keep silent also at congregational meetings? What about church school and vacation Bible school teachers? Should women sing in church choirs? How can we reconcile these oral and vocal activities with Paul's injunction for silence in the churches?

In 1 Corinthians 11 Paul based his injunctions regarding women covering their heads with a veil on the creation principle of male headship. If we take that principle to apply also to 1 Corinthians 14:34, then perhaps Paul is seeking to suppress female expressiveness in order to preserve marital relationships. Perhaps he is suggesting that female initiative and verbal participation in worship may undermine the husband–wife relationship at home. But Paul doesn't explicitly speak of headship in this passage.

Still this raises a question about the extent of the headship principle. Does it operate only in the sphere of marital (husband–wife) relationships or does it extend to *all* man–woman relationships?

In the original Greek language, you may recall, the words for male/man and female/woman are not easy to translate precisely. The choice often depends upon context, and the translation may be colored by how one interprets these words. Yet whether these terms are translated as man or husband or as woman or wife can strongly affect the meaning of headship.

If these words are taken to mean the headship of man over woman, thus not limiting headship to the husband–wife relationship, then it would seem to apply to all male-female relationships in every sphere of life—to worship, to church office, to education, to business, and to civil affairs. It would seem to extend across the board to all activities where men and women work, eat, play, or serve. It would seem to challenge, for example, the roles of Queen Beatrix of the Netherlands, Prime Minister Margaret Thatcher of England, and Justice Sandra O'Connor of the United States. And what about female principals in Christian schools or women on Christian school boards and denominational boards? May any of these women exercise authority over men?

A clear definition of headship seems as elusive as it is important. Recognizing this the Synod of 1981 appointed yet another study committee, this time "to examine the meaning and scope of headship in the Bible as it pertains to the relationships of husband and wife and man and woman..." (*Acts*, 1981, p. 98). Perhaps the results of this study will help us reach a united solution of the issue.

Learn in Silence?

1 Timothy 2:8–15

On the surface Paul appears to be telling women to say nothing in church. His words are very clear: "Let a woman learn in silence." However, the Greek word *hesuchia* (meaning "in quietness" or "in silence") doesn't mean a total absence of speech but rather a quiet, restrained demeanor (cf. Acts 22:2; 2 Thess. 3:12). A related word used in 1 Timothy 2:2 means "quiet" or "tranquil" (*Acts*, 1978, p. 523).

We must also probe the seeming contradiction in what Paul writes to Timothy and what he wrote to the Corinthian church concerning women keeping their heads covered while praying and prophesying. Again we need to consider Paul's intent in the entire letter.

Paul was writing to Timothy about members of a young church, some of whom were weak, all of whom were new to faith in Jesus Christ and to following his way. The excitement of conversion, the outpouring of the Holy Spirit, the headiness of communal loving and living, and the initial fervor of spreading the good news were beginning to subside and be replaced by some of the problems created by Christian weaknesses and shortcomings. It isn't hard to imagine that the Jewish Christians remained very alert to the goings-on in those new gentile Christian churches.

False teachers beguiled young believers. Some false leaders engaged in idle, meaningless chatter. Theologians of the law convinced the unwary of the importance of the law. Circumcision created a stumbling block for some. Others were offended by people eating meat that had been offered to idols. Women did not conduct themselves properly in church and neglected to show respect to the men. Confusion and irregularities marred the worship service itself.

Young Timothy, the pastor, needed instruction. Paul gave it, especially regarding worship. It seems appropriate to assume that Paul was speaking in this passage about the church and ecclesiastical assemblies, of "men praying in every place" (v. 8). (Look back at 1 Corinthians 14:33 to corroborate the idea that Paul is referring to public worship here.)

Paul's injunction to women to learn in silence reflects something needed to promote orderly conduct during the worship service. The principle involved seems clear. Conspicuous female consumers of Timothy's day were hurting the worship service by both their dress and speech. They lacked decorum and respect for the role of the husband/male. The principle of modesty and decorum in worship as expressed here is still in effect today.

Disagreement among Christians who study this issue today lies not in the principle but in the duration of the injunction. Was it temporary or permanent? To say it was temporary seems to make it relative to the time. To say it is a permanent restriction, that is, an injunction still valid today, raises the question of why we don't obey the parallel prohibitions against braided hair, gold and pearl jewelry, and expensive clothing for women.

Another area of disagreement involves: how we should translate the Greek words—as husband or man or as wife or woman? Paul says that women will be saved through child-bearing (v. 15). That seems to connote a marital, husband–wife, relationship. One could argue that this is what Paul means. Carrying it one step further, one might infer that Paul, as in 1 Corinthians 11, rests his teaching on the creational headship principle. Paul's comments here would seem to relate to headship in the marriage setting. But if this reasoning is correct and Paul's injunction is permanent, how will unmarried women be "saved"?

We sense again the need for a definition of headship and for settling the issue of whether this creational ordinance extends to all male–female relationships or simply to marriage.

An Overall Perspective

All who are debating this issue agree that women and men participate equally in the gifts of the Spirit. Baptism is administered equally to men and women. At the time of profession of faith, both are welcomed equally into the "full" communion of the church. In these matters, no disagreement exists.

But disagreement does exist on the meaning of this equality in the use of men's and women's gifts in the Christian community and in church office. Many serious Christians think that, in spite of our spiritual equality, the Bible enjoins a certain permanent subordination of woman to man. This, they say, extends far beyond the biblical description of the headship of man in a marriage relationship. Other serious Christians believe that any subordination, outside the mutual submissiveness of husband and wife in the marital relationship, resulted from the fall into sin in the Garden of Eden. Christ died on the cross to redeem humankind and creation. Therefore, Christians need to work together to remove the distortions and scars of sin wherever they occur. This includes all spheres of human relationships.

In synodical studies, discussions, and articles no agreement has been reached on which texts are to be considered *principles* and which are to be considered *applications* of principles. It is as though we cannot see the forest because of the trees. We are still "in the woods" rather than "out of the woods."

Perhaps it is time to step back from specific biblical texts and passages in order to clarify our overall perspective. We need to see clearly the overall picture: a beautiful, good creation; an ugly, devastating, and totally disrupting fall into sin; a glorious and liberating victory by the holy Savior; and a progression of the redeeming and reclaiming process until he comes again to finish what we have been unable to accomplish through him and for him in the restoration of a perfect creation. In such an overall perspective three thoughts might challenge us.

First, we need to give serious, deliberate, and methodical thought to the normativity of general revelation. The root word *norma* comes from Latin and means "a carpenter's square." Carpenters depend on squares as their authoritative standards or models. If they didn't, the finished building could prove unsightly or unreliable.

In the creation order God gives us the basic norms for human relationships, including those of male or husband and female or wife, in the various spheres of God's world. We need to focus clearly and sharply on a biblically directed and illumined doctrine of creation as the abiding foundation for *all* of life, including human relationships.

Second, we need to "hit the mark" with the questions we ask. Maybe we can't agree on an answer because we aren't asking the right question. We need to locate our questions concerning male–female relationships more self-consciously and deliberately within the biblical framework of creation, fall, and redemption on the way to the consummation of all things at the end of time.

Third, we need to rethink our handling of hermeneutic questions, to rethink our questions regarding interpretation of the Bible. Such questions must be raised within the comprehensive, indivisible perspective of a biblically Reformed world and life view. Life is a mosaic with many dimensions and a rich diversity to it. Yet running through it all is a deeply religious unity, held together by God's Word in Jesus Christ.

He is the image of the invisible God,
the first-born of all creation;
for in him all things were created,
in heaven and on earth,
visible and invisible,
whether thrones or dominions or principalities
   or authorities—
all things were created through him and for him.
He is before all things,
and in him all things hold together.

For in him all the fulness of God was pleased
   to dwell,
and through him to reconcile to himself all things,
whether on earth or in heaven,
making peace by the blood of his cross.

Colossians 1:15–17, 19–20

Study Session

First

As you know chapter 7 revolves around three key Pauline passages: Galatians 3:28, 1 Corinthians 14:33–36, and 1 Timothy 2:8–15. Reading these selections aloud will help set the stage for today's discussion. You may also wish to read Paul's great call for oneness in Christ, found in Ephesians 4:1–16.

Second

Choose from among the following discussion questions:

1. What principles of biblical interpretation have a particular bearing on the passages discussed in chapter 7?

2. Is Paul inconsistent? For example, compare 1 Corinthians 2:3 with 2 Corinthians 3:12. Or compare 1 Corinthians 11:5 with 1 Corinthians 14:34.

3. Explain why it is possible to claim too much support either for or against equal partnership in church work from Galatians 3:28.

4. Do you agree with the assertion in chapter 7 that Galatians 3:28 does "indirectly encourage us to consider whether all the gifts of women should not be used to help build the body of Christ to the coming of his kingdom (Eph. 4:1–16)"?

5. Chapter 7 suggests three ways of interpreting 1 Corinthians 14:33–36; of the three, which seems best to you?

How does the principle of headship relate to interpreting this passage?

6. Many women who marry today omit the "obey" promise of the marriage vow. In terms of oneness in Christ, is this an allowable omission or does it violate the creational principles of headship in marriage? Explain.

7. Can a relationship be equal if one partner is considered devoid of authority?

8. Do you think that Paul's injunction for women to "learn in silence" was of a temporary or permanent nature (1 Tim. 2:11)? Why? If permanent, then why don't we obey the parallel prohibitions against braided hair, jewelry, and expensive clothing for women? Comment.

Third

Take a moment to survey fellow class members on their feelings about the lack of consensus in the church on the passages discussed in today's lesson. Are you personally encouraged or discouraged at this time? How can a serious impasse in the churches be avoided, if at all?

Fourth

Having come this far in your study of the issue which faces us and our church, you have seen that the concepts and principles as interpreted by each position will require not only more discussion and study but also an enlightening and tolerant spirit of understanding from the Holy Spirit.

A concluding prayer:

Father in heaven,
we cannot understand that
you are Father, Son, and Holy Spirit.
Nor can we understand
how you answer prayers—
but we believe that you do
and you will.
Nor can we understand
how you may answer the prayer
of your children—
the issue troubles us,

the issue hurts and divides
our oneness in you;
some seek yes,
others seek no.
We are one
in your body,
troubled
at our inability
to see clearly
(as yet)
your answer.
Open our eyes
that we may see
a glimpse of the truth
we need from thee.
Open our hearts
to accept your will,
and let us hear
your "Peace, be still."
Amen.

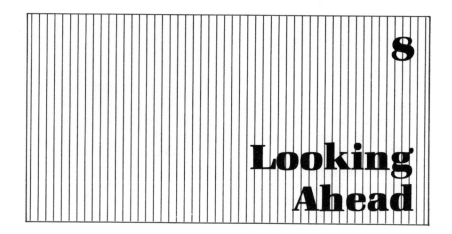

Looking Ahead

At the close of any unit of study the student should pause to evaluate. What has been learned? What objectives have been reached? You have used this book as a help in studying God's Word and in learning more about an issue that troubles our church. Paul reminded Timothy that "all Scripture is God-breathed and is useful for teaching, rebuking, correcting and training in righteousness" (2 Tim. 3:16 NIV). Have any of these scriptural objectives been reached in the study of this issue?

In this last lesson it may be helpful to review those questions on which consensus eludes us and those questions on which we seem to be moving toward certain basic agreements. Following this, we will conclude this study with some thoughts about looking and moving ahead.

Evaluating the Present

After a decade of intensive study, reflection, and discussion of the issue at hand, what position has the Christian Reformed Church reached? What areas of agreement and disagreement have been determined? Is it possible to isolate some principles or concepts on which enough consensus has been reached to allow us to hope for a future solution?

It seems that the synod has set aside, for the time being at least, the question of the permissibility of electing and installing women as elders or ministers. At the present time, then, we face the question: shall the office of deacon be opened to qualified women?

As yet there is no single answer in the church. Some say yes. Others say no. And even the *yes* folks disagree about how to implement such a move.

What is synod's position on women in office or on women as deacons? The 1978 decision still stands: to admit qualified women to the office of deacon. But synod has again deferred implementing that decision pending yet another committee, this one on the biblical idea of headship.

The present status of the issue may be summarized by considering areas in which consensus has and has not been achieved.

We have not achieved consensus on a clear understanding of whether the headship of man over woman means headship of *any* man over *any* woman in *every* sphere of life, or whether it means only the headship of husband over wife.

We have not reached consensus on an understanding of the pre-fall, post-fall, and redeemed relationship of man/husband to woman/wife.

We have not reached consensus on how to harmonize the biblical idea regarding the equal worth and spiritual equality of man and woman in the eyes of God with the other biblical idea concerning a certain subordination of the woman/wife to the man/husband.

We have not reached consensus on a definition of headship in its implications for ecclesiastical office.

We have not reached consensus on the specific biblical teaching regarding women in ecclesiastical office.

We have not reached consensus on how or how much contemporary issues should or should not shape our interpretation and application of biblical teachings.

We have not reached consensus on acceptable rules by which to reorganize the life of the church should women be admitted to the office of deacon.

Do you wonder, looking over the summary of matters on which consensus is lacking, whether this study has been worth your time and effort? Remind yourself that as a member of Christ's body you have a stake in the final decision and outcome. Issues should never be resolved without study and discussion. You may tire of synod's "apparent" delays, but because such issues do receive very thorough study, we may believe that synod's thoroughness has helped us conduct the King's business sincerely and wisely.

It would be discouraging if we believed the church has reached an impasse. So it is good, too, that we look at the areas in which we have achieved some consensus.

We seem to agree that there are no decisive biblical or theological reasons for excluding women from serving in the diaconate if certain Church Order questions can be answered. These questions, however, run rather deep. They concern not only the distinction between the tasks of deacons and elders but also the very nature of office in the church and the character of its authority.

We seem to agree that the word *deacon* (*diakonos* in Greek) always carries with it the idea of servant or service.

We seem to agree that in the New Testament the office of elder is more clearly defined than the office of deacon. The duties, tasks, and functions of early deacons seem rather uncertain. It's difficult to learn precisely from New Testament practice what the duties of today's deacons should be. In fact the Bible doesn't really offer a definite church order blueprint. We cannot identify today's diaconate with that of the New Testament. Neither can we trace the origin and institution of the office of deacon as we know it today directly and simply to the appointment of the seven in Acts 6.

We seem to agree that church history gives us no clear pattern for the office of deacon. History is, of course, in itself never normative, but we can still learn many valuable lessons from this record of more or less obedient responses to God's Word. But when we look at the almost 2,000-year story of the office of deacon, we get no clearly focused picture. Instead we find deacons performing a great variety of tasks:

preaching
teaching
baptizing
reading Scripture
leading in worship
hearing confessions
reconciling hostile parties
tending the dying
assisting bishops
performing wedding ceremonies

training for priesthood
visiting the sick, widows, orphans, and prisoners
caring for the poor, both spiritually and materially
administering church affairs

In addition, sometimes consistories appointed deacons; at other times the congregation elected them; occasionally town councils designated deacons. At times women were admitted to the diaconate; at other times and places they were not. In some cases deacons were included in the consistory together with ministers and elders; in other places, the diaconate was separate from the consistory. In some areas deacons were delegated to general assemblies.

The diaconate in church history presents a very mixed picture. Deacons seem to have been jacks- (and jills) of-all-trades. Many church leaders have taken the sort of flexible, practical approach to the question that John Calvin took, being willing to accommodate their understanding of diaconal work to local conditions and historical developments.

We seem to agree that as a general rule the church has assigned the task of caring for the poor to its deacons. Calvin considered this ministry of mercy to be the dominant mark of the office of the *diakonoi.*

We seem to agree that in the Christian Reformed tradition there are two lines of thought regarding the inclusion of deacons in or their exclusion from the consistory. The Church Order, like Calvin, distinguishes between diaconal and ruling offices. The Belgic Confession, however, counts deacons along with pastors and elders as part of the consistory.

Yet in spite of this consensus on certain matters, the church doesn't seem to agree on the direction in which it should move next. Some say the church needs its women in positions where their many gifts of intellect, leadership, and mercy may be more fully used. Others say we should drop the whole matter. The real dilemma facing the Christian Reformed Church is that neither going ahead to a rapid solution nor completely abolishing the issue is possible or realistic.

Looking Ahead

As we look and move ahead toward a consensus and solution for this issue, we should keep certain points in mind.

First, we should recognize that in the exercise of any office in the church, authority and service go hand in hand. Office, including the diaconate, rests upon a God-given authority. Anyone—whether he or she be pastor, elder, deacon, parent, teacher, or citizen—exercising the authority of his or her office is answerable to the Giver of that authority. Further, all office, with its authority and accountability, is for service to others and may never be used for self-aggrandizement.

Second, we should remember that in a very basic sense the four special offices we recognize in the church are ultimately not of the highest importance. Of fundamental importance is the office of *all* believers. The four church offices—deacon, elder, minister, and evangelist—are really specializations upon the general office of all believers. Church offices must serve the congregation and help equip all believers in the exercise of their various offices in society.

Third, although the office of evangelist was added by synod (1978) to the three offices of elder, minister, and deacon, the idea that the ecclesiastical offices basically constitute a *single* office is more than a "theological conjecture" (*Acts*, 1981, p. 365). Such a view ignores the historical development of the various offices in the church as reflected in the New Testament.

Considering the historical perspective of the unfolding biblical revelation within the New Testament, one can argue that the threefold office of pastor, elder, and deacon is rooted in and evolves from the single original apostolic office of the twelve apostles. From this one may reasonably affirm the basic unity and parity of all offices in the church. It would seem to follow then that what holds for one office also holds for the others—including the admission of qualified women.

Fourth, the implications of one threefold office, then, raise an urgent and pressing question. In essence, or in authority and dignity, can we or may we distinguish the office of deacon from that of elder? Or are they distinguishable only in task, duty, and function? And yet other questions follow from this. In the light of one threefold office, can the consistory and the diaconate legitimately be distinguished as two separate bodies? Can they be identified as general consistory and restricted consistory?

It would seem that at times, out of an earnest zeal and eagerness to follow the directions we derive from principles found in God's Word, we lose sight of the spirit and follow the letter. In the process of delineating the tasks and functions of offices in the church it may be that we have lost sight of the one threefold office.

Perhaps we have ecclesiasticized the biblical concept of office. That is, we have limited the biblical idea of office to the church and in so doing obscured office in other areas of life. Perhaps we have so narrowed the concept of office that we are able to recognize it only in the institutional church.

If the Christian Reformed Church has given the impression that no really important office exists except in the church, and then excludes women from such office, should we be surprised that half of the church's members—the women—feel left out?

A majority in our church seems ready to permit women to become deacons provided they, unlike the minister and elders, do not exercise ecclesiastical authority. This seems to suggest that the diaconate is not a decision-making body. But it is! It too acts with authority. The diaconate constantly uses authority to make decisions concerning goods, money, and people. Decision-making is necessary in the stewardship of gifts, both in the collection and the distribution of them.

Summary

In the days when people journeyed by horse, travelers needed guideposts and hitching posts. Both were important. Travelers not only had to know how to distinguish the two but also which post to use when.

Is the present issue, men and women as partners in service, a hitching post or a guidepost? If the question must be resolved on the basis of a permanent, basic biblical principle established in the early New Testament church, the issue is a hitching post. If, however, the question must find resolution on the basis of its being one application of a permanent, basic biblical principle established in the early

New Testament church, the issue is a guidepost.

The question for us then is to determine the basic character of this issue and the way in which it should be resolved. It is the prayer of the authors that this study book has served somewhat to that end.

Study
Session

First

The suggested Scripture reading is 1 Corinthians 12, a chapter which emphasizes our oneness and our need of each other. The verses are beautiful, comforting, and sobering.

Second

A few possibilities for discussion:

1. Chapter 8 describes certain areas of general disagreement (lack of consensus) and of agreement (at least a tendency toward consensus). Are there any areas in which you find yourself in sharp disagreement with this chapter's conclusions?

2. What lessons can we learn from the history of the diaconate? Consider especially John Calvin's position.

3. Does the idea of *servant* or *service* preclude the exercise of authority in office? Why or why not?

4. In what ways does the threefold office of believers comfort you? Challenge you? Frighten you?

5. Chapter 8 concludes by noting that the women's issue can be viewed as either a hitching post or a guidepost. Which is it to you? Why?

Third

The authors of this book hope that your study will extend beyond mere words into the area of personal and communal service to the church. Take a few moments, in closing, to discuss what you intend to do with what you've learned from this study and from other members of your group. Do you see it making any difference at all in your Christian life and in the life of the church?

A second question that could be discussed concerns goal achievement. Do you feel you realized your (personal or group) goals for this study?

Each group member should, ideally, be given time to respond to one or both of these questions.

Fourth

Since a summary of this book has already been given, none is required here. Yet the issue is urgent and tugs at the heartstrings of the church we all love. Peace comes from believing that God sees and knows the hearts of his people. Our prayer must be: "Your kingdom come." In closing this session pray the Lord's Prayer together.

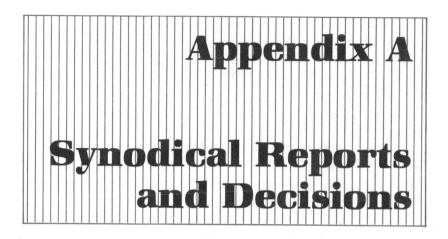

Appendix A

Synodical Reports and Decisions

A Brief History of the Women's Issue in the Christian Reformed Church

1914, 1916

Even while *Acts of Synod* were still being written in the Dutch language, the word *women* could be found in the index. At these sessions synod considered the question of women's suffrage in civic life, finally deciding that this was not an ecclesiastical matter.

1947

Classis Muskegon overtured synod to study and resolve the issue regarding the voting rights of women at congregational meetings. Classis Muskegon pointed out that the question not only related to the nature and proper function of the congregational meeting, but that it was also a matter of concern for the denomination as a whole, not just for individual consistories. Classis Muskegon stated also that some women members had requested the right to participate. Synod appointed a study committee of three pastors (Art. 96).

1950

Report on Proper Function of Congregational Meetings and Women's Vote (Report 20)

Synod agreed with the study committee (appointed in 1947) that it would be unwise to "make a pronouncement" because the "desired measure of agreement" couldn't be expected at that time. It asked the Reformed Ecumenical Synod (RES) to study the nature and authority of congregational meetings. Churches were advised to refuse women suffrage (Art. 109).

1954

Report from RES on Women Voting
at Congregational Meetings (Suppl. Report 41)

RES, in response to the Christian Reformed Church's request, said that women no less than men share in the gifts, rights, and obligations which Christ has given. Although men and women have different places and tasks in life, Paul, when he requires silence, addressed himself to married women so that they "should honor their God-given position with respect to their husbands," but he did not "impose silence on women in all spiritual and ecclesiastical matters."

Participation of women is not forbidden and withholding the right to vote may not be done on biblical grounds. A church, in giving or not giving women suffrage, must reckon seriously with local customs so that what is done may express not only the unity of man and woman in Christ but also their natural differences.

Synod appointed a committee to study and evaluate the Report from RES on Women Voting at Congregational Meetings (Art. 141).

1955

Report on Women Voting at Congregational Meetings
(Suppl. Report 7)

The synodical study committee pointed out that the request by the Synod of 1950 had specifically been about the nature and authority of congregational meetings and the RES had not taken cognizance of this fact. Therefore the committee recommended that another study committee be appointed, a committee which would study the Report of 1950, together with the Reports of 1930 and 1952 of the Gerefermeerde Kerken in the Netherlands. The study should deal specifically with the question of women suffrage in congregational meetings.

Accordingly synod appointed a committee to study the Report of 1950, together with the Reports of 1930 and 1952 of the Gerefermeerde Kerken, and to make recommendations to the Synod of 1956 or 1957 (Art. 74).

1957

Women Suffrage in Ecclesiastical Meetings
(Suppl. Report 19)

The study committee recommended unanimously that women be enfranchised at congregational meetings. One member of the committee in a separate addendum suggested that nonparticipation shouldn't be considered a violation of a specific biblical directive.

Synod decided that women may vote in congregational meetings, subject to the rules that govern the participation of men. Questions of *whether* and *when* women should be invited to participate were left to the judgment of each consistory (Art. 155).

1958

Protest from Classis Minnesota North on
Women Suffrage in Congregational Meetings (Report 3)

The classis protested synod's approval of women suffrage on the grounds that no "Scriptural, creedal, or constitutional" grounds were offered to the "radically new concept" of women voting. The classis also said that the congregational meeting's purpose is to assist in the governing of the congregation.

Synod, in response to the protest from Classis Minnesota North, said that the church doesn't recognize the congregational meeting as an ecclesiastical assembly and that the action of Synod of 1957 was based on Scripture. Synod, therefore, rejected the protest (Art. 85).

1969

Synod appointed a committee to "study the nature of ecclesiastical office and the meaning of ordination as taught in the Bible" and as seen in church history. Synod said that an RES Report of 1968 didn't answer the basic question of whether there is a "basic created natural place and function of women subservient to men" (Art. 121).

1970

Because the RES Report of 1968 had shown a sharp disagreement with CRC Church Order on the issue of women holding office in the church, synod appointed a committee to examine, in the light of Scripture, the general practice of excluding women from church office (Art. 167).

1972

Report on Ecclesiastical Office and Ordination
(Report 40)

Prepared by the committee appointed in 1969, this report recommended, among other matters, that:

1. The word *office* means "service" or "ministry" and embraces the total ministry of the church.
2. This comprehensive office, this ministry of Christ, is universal and is committed to the whole church, not to a select group of individuals within the church.
3. Some individuals may be designated for special tasks or services or ministries.
4. These special ministries are functional and are characterized by service rather than status or dominance.
5. Special or particular ministries are distinguishable by function but are in essence identical. "There is therefore no essential distinction but only a functional one between ministers, elders, deacons, and all other members of the church."
6. Preaching the Word and administering the sacraments are not tasks "explicitly limited to special office holders.... The church assigns these functions to certain individuals...with a view to maintaining good order...so that it may carry out its ministry most effectively."
7. The Bible leaves room for the church to adapt or modify its special ministries in order to carry out Christ's mandate "effectively in all circumstances."

Synod sent the Report on Ecclesiastical Office and Ordination back to the committee for additional study. Synod asked, "Was Christ's authority delegated to his whole church or to special offices or to both?" Synod sought also to know the nature of the authority involved in special office and the nature of the relationship between the task and authority of the apostles and that of other offices in the church (Art. 69).

Overture from Classis Hudson on Women at Congregational Meetings (Report 14)

Classis Hudson asked synod to declare that women are called to participate and vote in congregational meetings. Voting is not merely a right; therefore, individual consistories shouldn't make judgments on the matter.

Overture from Winnipeg College Avenue CRC on Women at Congregational Meetings (Report 30)

Winnipeg College Avenue CRC consistory asked synod not to accede to the overture of Classis Hudson.

In response to these overtures regarding women participating in congregational meetings, synod reiterated its stated position of 1957. Synod encouraged consistories which didn't allow women to vote to reconsider the matter seriously. However, it rejected Classis Hudson's request that all women be enfranchised (Art. 74).

1973

Report on Ecclesiastical Office and Ordination (Report 44)

This is an extension of 1972's report of the same title (Report 40) which had been reassigned to the study committee for further work. In addition to the earlier report it specifically answered synod's questions on the nature of authority, forms for ordination, and questions related to the Belgic Confession. It concluded that "the authority which is associated with special ministries is an authority defined in terms of love and service."

Synod adopted the recommendations contained in the Report on Ecclesiastical Office and Ordination (Report 44). These in essence repeated the recommendations of a similar report (Report 40) in 1972 (Art. 64).

Report on Women in Ecclesiastical Office
(Report 39)

The committee, assigned a mandate in 1970, concluded that:

1. The practice of excluding women from office cannot be conclusively defended on biblical grounds.
2. A summary of the Bible's teaching on this principle is:
   a) Christ's redemption and restoration results in oneness of the sexes and does not allow for discrimination.
   b) The Bible warns "against the idea of sameness between the sexes."
   c) In biblical history many women have held office.
   d) Scripture stresses the *modus* ("way") in which women should function in the church. This *modus* may not give offense and should be conducive to the ministry of the church.
3. The question of women in office should be studied in light of the above.
4. Synod should appoint another committee to study whether the word *male* in Church Order Article 3 should be deleted.

One member of the committee couldn't agree with all the recommendations. His Postscript may be found in *Acts of Synod 1973* (pp. 588–94).

Because of the nature and comprehensiveness of the Report on Women in Ecclesiastical Office and the effect its adoption would have on church policy, synod deferred action until all churches could study the matter. It stated that several issues needed further study, issues including principles of interpretation, the creation order and its implications, the meaning of headship, and the concepts of masculinity and femininity.

Synod appointed a new committee to study the place and role of women in the church and to receive and evaluate the reaction of the churches to Report 39 (Art. 81).

1974

Synod charged the committee studying "Women in Ecclesiastical Office" to consider the distinction between licensure and ordination, and exhorting and preaching, because this distinction might bear on the place of women in the seminary's field education (Art. 32).

1975

Report on Women in Office
(Report 46)

The study committee reported the results of its survey and their analysis of that data. It recommended a statement to the effect that "the Christian Reformed Church is not ready or willing to open her offices to women."

It also concluded that in principle the Bible is not opposed to "the ordination of women to any office that men may hold in the church." The Bible does teach that any new practice must uphold the authority structure within marriage and the support this structure derives from existing practices must not be weakened.

The committee urged the churches to make all possible use (within biblical guidelines and Church Order) of women's gifts. One committee member had some reservations about the report (see *Acts of Synod 1975*, pp. 593–94).

Synod decided to continue excluding women from ecclesiastical office "unless compelling biblical grounds are advanced for changing that practice." It also noted that no such biblical grounds had been advanced.

Synod further urged churches to make all possible use (within biblical guidelines) of women's gifts and talents. It appointed a committee of men and women to help the churches implement that advice.

Further, synod assigned a committee to study the hermeneutical principles involved in interpreting relevant passages and to apply them to the texts and passages in question (Art. 79).

1976

Report on Women in Ecclesiastical Office
(Report 44)

The committee, recognizing that synod's 1975 decision to

maintain the practice of excluding women from ordination made their work unnecessary, recommended that synod lay aside its mandate to the committee.

Synod withdrew its mandate given to a committee in 1974 to define the differences between licensure and ordination, and exhorting and preaching (Art. 51).

1978

Report on Hermeneutical Principles Concerning Women in Church Office (Report 31)

Although the study committee experienced some difficulty with the imprecision of its mandate and with the question of historical context, it concluded that man and woman have equality of worth as God's imagebearers. Restricting the conduct of a group of believers (women) should be done only "on the basis of unambiguously clear Biblical evidence."

An element of authority is involved in the God-established relationship of husband and wife which was instituted before humanity's fall into sin. The church must uphold this headship in marriage.

The New Testament affirms and develops the idea of full participation of women in the gifts of the Spirit and the work of the church. The New Testament equality of man and woman was demonstrated by replacing circumcision with baptism. The New Testament didn't, however, permit wives, by either appearance or deportment, to contradict the marital headship of their husbands.

Synod decided that consistories may ordain qualified women as deacons, provided their work is distinguished from that of elders.

It also agreed to amend Church Order Article 3 so that it would conform to the permission granted for qualified ordination of women as deacons. Synod then asked Synod of 1979 to ratify this change in Church Order Article 3 (Art. 80).

Report of Service Committee for Use of Members' Gifts (Report 36)

The committee reported that to foster the wider use of members' gifts it had sent out letters to consistories, adopted the idea of a referral data bank, proposed to *The Banner* that it start a column regarding these gifts, and encouraged conferences on this subject.

Appeal of the Church of the Servant of the Decision of the Calvin Board of Trustees (Report 2)

This appeal to synod to examine Marchiene Rienstra and declare her to be a candidate for the ministry of the Christian Reformed Church was considered by the advisory committee. While recognizing that "with respect to her doctrinal soundness, spiritual fitness and personality . . . Marchiene is well qualified for Christian ministry," the committee recommended that synod declare the Board of Trustees had acted properly (according to Church Order Art. 3) in not permitting her candidacy.

Synod adopted this recommendation, advising the Church of the Servant "to encourage Mrs. Rienstra to use her gifts within the guidelines of Scripture and the Church Order in the CRC" (Art. 84).

1979

Synod noted that several consistories had ordained women to the office of deacon. Synod also received overtures, appeals, and communications from various churches and individuals asking for clarification, for deferment of ratification of synod's 1978 decision on the Church Order, or for rescinding the 1978 decision.

Synod decided to defer its decision on ratifying the new wording of Church Order Article 3 and instructed consistories to defer implementing the 1978 decision. Synod also appointed another study committee, mandated to study "without prejudice" the 1978 Report 31 (on hermeneutical principles) and Article 80.

Synod asked the committee particularly to concentrate on "the office of deacon in the light of Church Order Article 35," giving specific attention to the idea of "male headship and the nature of that authority" (Art. 97).

1980

Because some churches had ordained women as deacons as a result of synod's 1978 decision but prior to the rescinding of that action in 1979 by synod, the Synod of 1980 directed that these women be permitted to finish the terms for which they were elected.

Synod reminded all consistories that they are not to "elect or ordain women as deacons until further decision by Synod" (Art. 66).

1981

Synodical Studies on Women in Office and Decisions Pertaining to the Office of Deacon (Report 32)

Synod didn't accept the Majority Report or the Minority Reports 1 and 2 or its own Advisory Committee's recommendations. It was the recommendation of an ad hoc committee regarding church order and women in office that won synodical approval.

Synod decided to postpone implementing the 1978 decision pending the finding of a new study committee it appointed to examine the meaning and scope of the biblical principle of headship (Art. 125).

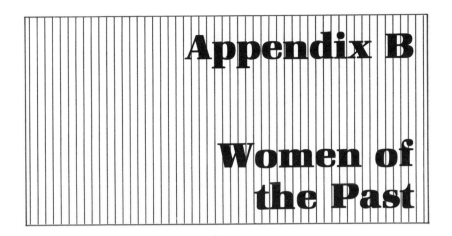

Women of the Bible*

Deborah was a judge and was considered a hero during the period when Israel was ruled by judges. Her leadership ability was demonstrated when she rallied the men of Israel to fight the Canaanites who had been tormenting them for many years (Judg. 4 & 5).

Elizabeth was a sincere woman of Israel, married to the priest Zechariah. They were a childless couple, yet the shame of being childless was usually associated with the woman. God finally sent them a son, John (known in Bible history as "the Baptist"), in their old age. When Elizabeth was six months pregnant, God used her to comfort Mary, the mother-to-be of Jesus (Luke 1).

Esther was first chosen because of her beauty to replace the Persian queen and later chosen by her uncle (through God's providence) to thwart Haman's plan to annihilate the Jews. Esther risked her life to save her people; she interceded with the king who listened to her. Her uncle's question, "Who knoweth but that thou art not come to the Kingdom for such a time as this?" still rings in the ears of those who remember not merely her beauty but her bravery (Book of Esther).

Eunice was an early New Testament Christian, married to a non-Jew. We remember Eunice through her son Timothy who was taught the Old Testament by Eunice and his grandmother Lois (Acts 16:1; 2 Tim. 1:5; 3:14–15).

---

*Information taken from William P. Barkar, *Everyone in the Bible*.

Eve, the first woman, bore a name which in Hebrew meant "life-giving"; she was the mother of humankind. Eve disobeyed God's command not to eat of a certain tree in the garden; she encouraged her husband Adam to eat also. This was the infamous fall into sin, the source of all estrangement between God and people, nations and races, brothers and sisters (Gen. 3:20; 4:1; 2 Cor. 11:3; 1 Tim. 2:13).

Huldah was the wife of the king's wardrobe keeper (hardly a position of renown or esteem). When a scroll containing what we now know as Deuteronomy was found, King Josiah immediately sent it to Huldah for explanation. Huldah prophesied an early day of reckoning for Israel, postponed only because of King Josiah's faith and fear of God and his desire that his people turn to God (2 Kings 22:14–20).

Lois was the mother of Eunice (see *Eunice*).

Mary and her sister *Martha* often provided Jesus with hospitality—all of which takes time in the kitchen. Mary preferred to spend time listening to and talking with Jesus, while Martha worked. When Martha objected, Jesus commended Mary for her choice of what was more essential (Luke 10:38–42; John 11:1–45; 12:1–8).

Mary Magdalene was healed of seven demons by Jesus. She became part of Jesus' entourage; she provided money and provisions to Jesus and accompanied the group on tour. She witnessed Jesus' death. She was the first person to whom Jesus showed himself after he arose from the dead (Matt. 27:55–61; Mark 15:40–47; Luke 8:1–3; John 20:1–18).

Mary, mother of Jesus, may have suffered both loneliness and embarrassment because of her early pregnancy. To become the mother of the Messiah was every Jewish girl's dream, but pain and hurt accompanied the joy. She was with the believers at the time Jesus arose and is generally remembered and honored as the mother of Jesus (Matt. 1 & 2; Luke 1 & 2).

Miriam, older sister of Moses and Aaron, was known as a prophetess. She wrote a song of praise after the Israelites defeated the Egyptians at the time of the Red Sea crossing. She exceeded her authority when she criticized Moses for his interracial marriage. God punished her with leprosy and later cured her after she asked for forgiveness. The name Mary, a derivation of Miriam's name, is an indication of the esteem in which she was held by her nation (Ex. 15:20–21;

Num. 12:1–15).

Phoebe was a Corinthian deaconess. Paul praised her for her kindness to the people at Cenchreae in Corinth (Rom. 16:1–2).

Priscilla was a leader in her church. She and her husband Aquila had been expelled from Rome and moved to Corinth, where they became strong supporters of Paul. They worked with him and traveled with him. She and Aquila corrected errors in Apollos's teaching. Later they moved back to Rome, then to Ephesus. Priscilla's name began to take on more prominence than her husband's name (Acts 18:2–3, 18, 26; Rom. 16:3–4; 1 Cor. 16:19; 2 Tim. 4:19).

Ruth was a Moabitess who married a Jew (Boaz), and from this family both David and Jesus descended. Although she was not a Jew, God called and engrafted her into the Jewish family. Ruth demonstrated her love and loyalty when she wouldn't leave her mother-in-law, Naomi, who, completely disillusioned because of death, poverty, and famine, returned to Israel from Moab (Book of Ruth; Matt. 1:5).

Sarah, wife of Abraham, the father of the covenant, went with Abraham from a land of high civilization to the strange land of Canaan and later to Egypt. Sarah suffered personal grief because of being childless. After urging Abraham to have a son by her maid Hagar, Sarah turned against her maid. Later Sarah became the mother of Isaac, through whom God continued the covenant (Gen. 11:29–31, 12, 16–18, 20–21, 23; Heb. 11:11).

Women of History

Tena Huizinga was a member of the Christian Reformed Church who gave her life to the Nigerians of Africa. As a medical missionary, Miss Huizinga was a *baturiya* ("white lady") of medicine and a bearer of the good news of salvation to all who knocked at her door. No one was ever turned away—all received help for physical and/or spiritual ills.

Joan of Arc, the Maid of Orleans, a fifteenth-century heroine, was burned at the stake for witchcraft. She previously had rallied the dispirited French soldiers to defeat the English at Orleans.

Monica is remembered as the mother who wouldn't cease praying for her unbelieving son, Augustine. Later he was converted and thanked his mother for her unflagging prayers for him. Augustine became one of the church's outstanding men of God.

Mother Teresa spends her life ministering to dying beggars on the crowded streets of Calcutta, India. She won the 1979 Nobel Peace Prize for her unstinting charity and selflessness. When asked why she gave all her time and talent to people who would soon die, she replied, "God doesn't ask me to be successful; he asks me only to be faithful."

Ruth Vander Meulen served the people of Nigeria for twenty-five years as a medical missionary of the Christian Reformed Church. She left the mission field and returned to the United States in 1980. While in Nigeria, she was known for her superb midwifery abilities, demonstrated in the name of our merciful Christ, in a land where many mothers do not yet know the elementary facts of prenatal and postnatal hygiene.

Johanna Veenstra was called by God to preach to blacks in Nigeria. Constant obstacles didn't daunt her. She is the Christian Reformed Church's example of a woman called by God to preach to his imagebearers. She gave her life for God.

Suzannah Wesley preached many sermons. The significance of her preaching is enhanced when one notes that she mothered seventeen children and managed to spend one private hour per week with each child.

Queen Wilhelmina of the House of Orange was Queen of the Netherlands during World War II when the Dutch suffered so much at the hands of the Nazis.

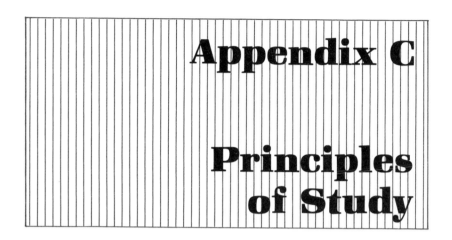

Appendix C

Principles of Study

The Bible is infallible and speaks with full authority as it reveals God's will to us personally and communally in his words and acts (Matt. 5:17–18; 1 Cor. 2:14; 2 Tim. 3:16–17).

Christians in the Reformed, Calvinistic tradition gladly accept this truth. In fact, belief in this principle is one of the basic reasons why equality and partnership for men and women is an issue in the Christian Reformed denomination. We ask and know that the Bible speaks to us with authority; yet an understanding of the intent of that authoritative speaking is essential. If the Bible's *intention* is not rightly understood, its *authority* may be misdirected and misunderstood; and then its authority has vanished. One day when Jesus preached in the mountains he said, "...When you pray, go into your room and shut the door.... When you fast, anoint your head and wash your face..." (Matt. 6:6, 17). This is not a literal command to go to our room and shut the door or to pour oil on our heads, but the *intention* is clear. If its intended meaning escapes us, the Bible ceases to function (at that point) as God's authoritative Word in our lives.

After creation and the fall, the Bible brings us a redemptive message to liberate and renew our lives.

Hallelujah for that! Have you ever tried to imagine an Old Testament without the promise of Genesis 3:15? Without the story of the Jews and their astonishing relationship with God at a time in history when the idea of one God was absurd? Without the inclusion of people like Jacob, Noah, Rahab, Samuel, Rachel, Deborah, Samson, and David? Without the evidence of the stunning providence of God in the stories of Ruth and Esther? Without the promise of a Redeemer?

An organic unity of purpose and a definite development or progression runs through all the diversity of the Bible. It is important that Christians see the continuity and discontinuity (promise and fulfillment) between the Old and New Testaments and the development of revelation.

The redemption story coincides with the history of the development of God's kingdom. The kingdom begins with creation in Adam; it falls and its restoration begins; with the calling of Israel it is established as a nation. Sorrow multiplies when the kingdom divides and falls and its people scatter. After 400 dark years the King himself comes, and after his death and resurrection the Holy Spirit expands this kingdom to every spot on the globe. Now we await his return!

Can any story compete with the power and majesty of such liberation and renewal? Can any story match such continuing mercy on the part of King Jesus?

Another interesting aspect of this organic unity is the progress in revelation. What is foreshadowed implicitly becomes explicit later. With the fullness of revelation we have today, it is hard to imagine one's religious understanding being limited to what the Israelites read on the Sabbath or, if you were fortunate enough to be a boy, to what you read of the law! The old saying, "The New is in the Old concealed; the Old is in the New revealed," is a simple way to express the organic unity of the Bible.

The Bible as Word of God is thoroughly historical in its use of the language, imagery, literary forms, and thought patterns of its day.

Do you have some uneasiness when you hear that archaeologists and anthropologists have just uncovered new artifacts or writings in Palestine? You need not. As scholars refine their research methods they generally confirm the historicity of biblical events, cities, kings, customs, and thought patterns. Just recently a magazine carried a small item confirming, it said, the place where God "drowned the obstinate Pharaoh and all his host in the Red Sea" and "led his people Israel through the midst of the sea upon dry ground."

The Bible is true to its day. If the Bible were to be written today by persons inspired by God to write infallibly, living in the heart of an enormous cosmopolitan metropolis in North America, its parables, language, imagery, and thought patterns would reflect, no doubt, the Bible's message in forms which the twentieth-century urbanite would better understand. Then perhaps the issue being studied here wouldn't even exist.

In interpreting the Bible we must take seriously not only the historical but also the literary and theological elements within the text of Scripture itself.

The Bible uses literature in ways that are still common today. Several types stand out: narrative, poetry, letters (epistles), prophecies, parables, laws, history. It also uses several literary devices: metaphors, similes, parallelisms, alliterations, and word plays. Recognizing and understanding some of these devices, the metaphor for example, is helpful in interpretation. When the poet described his enemies, he said, "They surrounded me like bees, they blazed like a fire of thorns" (Ps. 118:12). The poet's desperation is easy to visualize. We sense the pain.

Theological elements, of course, are of primary concern to us as we seek to hear God speak. Not all passages of the Bible are equally close to the central purpose, but all are God's revelation to us. The questions we must ask are, "What is *God* saying? How is God *revealing* himself here?"

The answers we seek are not dependent on one but on all elements that enter in, including the literary and theological. The Bible isn't a textbook, a science manual, or an encyclopedia, but a proper interpretation of the Bible compels us to consider all the elements which contribute to its richness.

Often the Bible speaks polemically (in refutation of), fighting against errors which threaten the life of God's people, and at other times it reflects God's accommodating himself to the practices of the day.

Sometimes the Bible seems to accommodate itself to the social patterns of the times. For example, polygamy was tolerated in the Old Testament (see Deut. 21:15–17 and the stories of Jacob and Abraham). But at other times, evil is bluntly opposed (the Israelites were specifically forbidden to follow practices of their Canaanite neighbors).

Proper interpretation demands that we determine whether a biblical command or injunction applies only to a specific situation or to believers everywhere and in every era.

Of utmost importance is the principle of the analogy of Scripture, that is, comparing Scripture with Scripture.

People who don't enjoy the God-given gift of faith that enables the Bible reader to read and absorb God's Word wonder aloud about apparent inconsistencies. These so-called discrepancies and seeming contradictions puzzle Christians too at times. Louis Berkhof (*Principles of Interpretation,* p. 166) teaches students to bear in mind that the contrary and obscure passage shouldn't diminish a doctrine "clearly supported by faith." He further states that when Scripture supports two doctrines that appear contradictory (as so many argue is the case with divine sovereignty and human responsibility) "both should be accepted as scriptural in the confident belief that they resolve themselves into a higher unity."

In dealing with various passages, we must distinguish between abiding principles (which are always normative) and specific applications (which are related to certain historical situations).

We need no reminder that recognition or lack of recognition of this difference has given birth to many groups of believers over the past twenty centuries. It has created differences within churches as well (e.g., the holy kiss, baptism, hats and veils, use of musical instruments, wine or grape juice, Sunday observances, length of hair, worldly amusements).

The Bible can be so very specific—and so very general. Often concrete applications are provided for specific occasions. It is rather easy to consider some text to be a moral principle rather than merely the application of a moral principle. Care needs to be exercised that the principle and not the specific culture-bound application is the basis for discussions today.